"The importance of gospel rhythms for litu
be overstated. This Lenten guide will take yo
Easter through readings from Scripture, confe
devotionals, and questions for reflection. Pre|
journey to the cross."

    Gregg R. Allison, Professor of Christian Theology, The Southern Baptist
Theological Seminary

"This is the most helpful resource for Lent I have found. If you are looking for
something to guide you through the Lent season—to serve as a tool of preparation
and repentance as you immerse in the story of the gospel—I highly recommend
this guide."

    Ben Peays, Executive Director, The Gospel Coalition

"In one of my favorite hymns, Isaac Watts invites us to 'survey the wonders of the
cross.' Many thanks to Kendal Haug and Will Walker, for helping us enter that grace-
laden exploration. *Journey to the Cross* is the newest, and now the finest, devotional
resource in my library for the season of Lent. These daily meditations will help
you see more of the beauty of Jesus; understand afresh the depth of your need; and
marvel at the immeasurable riches of grace—freely ours, through the costly work
of the cross. Thank you, my brothers, for helping me understand a little better, what
'boasting in the cross' is all about. Buy a copy for yourself, and several for friends."

    Scotty Ward Smith, Teacher in Residence, West End Community Church

"If you're skeptical of Lent, if you doubt the relevance of the church calendar
for gospel-loving Christians, this resource is for you. Will and Kendal helped
awaken me to the richness of the Lenten season as a time for gospel renewal. This
isn't stuffy, archaic liturgy; it's gospel-saturated reflection that will deepen your
affection for Christ."

    Bob Thune, Founding Pastor of Coram Deo Church; author of *Gospel
Eldership*; coauthor of *The Gospel-Centered Life*

"*Journey to the Cross* makes Lent accessible and meaningful to those unfamiliar
with its place in the Christian calendar. Its simple structure, biblical focus, and
reflective tone make it a spiritually formative tool to anticipate the sin-forgiving,
death-defeating, and evil-trouncing event of the resurrection."

    Jonathan K. Dodson, Founding Pastor of City Life Church; author
of *Gospel-Centered Discipleship, Raised? Finding Jesus by Doubting the
Resurrection*, and *The Unbelievable Gospel: Say Something Worth Believing*

"With their Lenten devotional, Will Walker and Kendal Haug have beautifully
answered questions Protestant disciples often ask: What is Lent? How should I
observe Lent? *Journey to the Cross* is a wise, pastoral, and Christ-centered approach
to Lent. It focuses on Jesus's journey to the cross. It points to Jesus's love, devotion,
and sacrifice, and so enriches our preparation to receive his gracious redemption."

    Dan Doriani, Professor and Vice President, Covenant Theological Seminary

JOURNEY TO THE CROSS

Devotions for Lent

Will Walker and Kendal Haug

New Growth Press
newgrowthpress.com

New Growth Press, Greensboro, NC 27401
Copyright © 2017 Will Walker and Kendal Haug

All rights reserved. No part of this publication may be reproduced, stored in a retrieval system, or transmitted in any form by any means, electronic, mechanical, photocopy, recording, or otherwise, without the prior permission of the publisher, except as provided by USA copyright law.

Scripture quotations are taken from The Holy Bible, English Standard Version.® Copyright © 2000; 2001 by Crossway Bibles, a division of Good News Publishers. Used by permission. All rights reserved.

Cover Design: Faceout Books, faceoutstudio.com

ISBN 978-1-945270-02-4 (Print)
ISBN 978-1-945270-03-1 (eBook)

Library of Congress Cataloging-in-Publication Data

Names: Walker, Will, 1975- author.
Title: Journey to the cross : devotions for Lent / Will Walker and Kendal Haug.
Description: Greensboro, NC : New Growth Press, 2017. | Includes bibliographical references and index.
Identifiers: LCCN 2016051898 | ISBN 9781945270024 (trade paper)
Subjects: LCSH: Lent--Prayers and devotions.
Classification: LCC BV85 .W3155 2017 | DDC 242/.34--dc23
LC record available at https://lccn.loc.gov/201605189824

Printed in India

28 27 26 25 24 23 22 21   4 5 6 7 8

Contents

Foreword

The Lenten Season in the early church was the prelude to the most important celebration in the church's calendar, the greatest event of all history, the culmination of the incarnation, the death of death procured in the death of Jesus Christ (and subsequently evidenced by the empty tomb three days later). Early Christians prepared for these events by stepping out of their normal routine for special times of devotion, prayer and sacrifice, focusing their minds and hearts on the meaning and implications of Calvary.

While the centuries have passed and some traditions have changed, the "Easter Event," encompassing the redeeming event through Christ and his triumph, with significant implications for us, remains extremely significant. In the facilitation of that celebration, the work before you is a wonderful tool to assist any Christian regardless of traditional background. Let me explain why this volume can be of significant benefit to you spiritually as you and your family prepare for the celebration of Jesus's death.

First, what follows is a daily devotional guide that walks through each day of the Lenten Season as preparation for that "dark" Friday and "glorious" Sunday. The structure follows the traditional pattern of Scripture readings, prayer, confession, and exposition of a text, followed by application questions. It is skillfully designed and reader accessible. Second, the quality of each daily devotional, encompassed in two pages, is markedly poignant, doctrinally accurate, and well constructed literarily. Third, this type of devotional literature, that seeks to reinstate the historic celebrations in the Christian calendar, goes a long way in rooting Christians in a rich heritage that has been eroded over recent centuries by modern and postmodern impulses.

I found reading it a delight to my mind and refreshment to my soul.

John D. Hannah
Distinguished Professor of Historical Theology; Research Professor of Theological Studies, Dallas Theological Seminary

Introduction

What Is Lent?

Lent is first and foremost about the gospel making its way deeper into our lives. This season is an opportunity to root ourselves in the good news that God saves sinners through the life, death, and resurrection of Jesus. It is a time to take stock, examine our hearts, repent of sin, turn to God, reflect on the suffering our Savior endured to accomplish our salvation, and finally rest in the assurance of that salvation.

Observing Lent is not necessary or central to experiencing life in Christ. Furthermore, this is not a season of "doing penance." Rather, having been sealed in Christ with the Holy Spirit, Lent is a season where we intentionally set aside time to remember Jesus and the grace that is found through faith in him alone. Lent is not about our faithfulness, but rather about the faithfulness of Jesus on our behalf.

Lent is the season leading up to Easter. We are all familiar with the celebration of Easter, and even the somber reflection of Good Friday. But Lent is an extended time of repentance and preparation leading up to those two days. In the fourth century, the church marked the beginning of Lent by counting back forty days from Easter (excluding Sundays), which takes you to the Wednesday seven weeks before Easter. Sundays themselves are not counted in these forty days, as they are generally set aside as days of renewal and celebration ("mini-Easters" of sorts).

The number forty carries great biblical significance. There were the forty days of rain that Noah and his family endured in the flood, the forty years that Israel spent in the wilderness, Jesus's forty-day fast in the wilderness, and the forty days Jesus spent on the earth after his resurrection. The time period of forty days was used by God to represent periods of trial, testing, and preparation.

Likewise, Lent is a season of preparation and repentance during which we anticipate the death (Good Friday) and resurrection (Easter Sunday) of Jesus. It is this preparation and repentance—aimed at grasping the intense significance of the crucifixion—that gives us a deep and powerful longing for the resurrection, the joy of Easter.

As the title of this devotional suggests, Lent is a journey to the cross: meditating on our sin and weakness, looking to Jesus as our perfect example and substitute, and being thankful for his victory over Satan, sin, and death. On the cross, Jesus took our place to appease God's righteous anger toward our sin and rebellion. He was cursed by God so that we could be blessed by God. He was forsaken by God so that we could be adopted by God. He was raised with God so that we too might walk in newness of life.

The journey of Lent is to immerse ourselves in this grand story so that it might increase our appreciation of Easter and love for Jesus. Throughout this journey, may we continually be "looking to Jesus, the founder and perfecter of our faith, who for the joy that was set before him endured the cross, despising the shame, and is seated at the right hand of the throne of God" (Hebrews 12:2).

How to Use This Book

This book is a devotional guide for the season of Lent. Each day consists of Scripture readings, meditations, reflection questions, and prayers—all aimed toward directing your heart to God and deepening your understanding of the events that led to Easter.

Each week of the devotional is focused on a different theme: repentance, humility, suffering, lament, sacrifice, and death. Although not exclusive to Lent, these themes capture the content and tone of the season. They point us to Jesus, and to put it simply, Lent is about Jesus. Our aim is to reflect meaningfully on his journey to the cross, so that we might take up our cross and follow him. Every day will follow a distinct pattern:

Daily Readings

CALL TO WORSHIP

Worship starts with God. He calls us into his presence, and we respond by coming before him in faith. Each day in this guide begins with a *Call to Worship*, which is generally a Scripture reading or Psalm that directs our focus to God as the initiator of our salvation and our covenant Lord. Use these passages to orient your heart and mind toward him.

CONFESSION

As we consider the greatness of a holy God and experience his presence in our lives, we are mindful of our sin and idolatry. God does not turn us away, but invites us to confess our sins and be cleansed. This is a normal rhythm of worship, but during Lent we have a heightened sense of our deep need for forgiveness. Use these moments each day as a way to walk humbly before God and deepen your desire to live in the light with him.

THE GOSPEL OF MARK

Reading straight through Mark's gospel account (starting with Peter confessing Jesus as the Christ) will provide not only a backdrop for our own Lenten journey, but also a reminder of the grander story we are a part of every day. Read these narrative sections as a way to immerse yourself in the life of Jesus and his journey to the cross.

PRAYER OF THANKSGIVING

Simple prayers of thanksgiving remind us of the forgiveness we have through Jesus and our new life in the Spirit. We are cleansed and sustained by him alone.

Daily Devotion

This section begins with a Scripture passage and devotional writings that touch on some aspect of that week's theme. As you begin this portion of the devotional each day, pray that God would speak to you through his Word and Spirit.

REFLECTION QUESTIONS

These questions flow directly out of the devotional and are intended to press us deeper into repentance and faith in Jesus. Approach these questions each day with this simple mindset: How is God speaking to you, and how do you want to respond? The journey is a Spirit-led journey, so learn to trust his leading and power in your life.

CLOSING PRAYER

Using the words from various liturgical resources, these prayers close each day as an added way to commune with God and express your desire to be transformed by his Spirit.

A word about Sundays: Sundays in Lent are intended as a foretaste of Easter Sunday—they are "mini-Easters." This guide includes professions (statements) of faith in Christ and hymns about his resurrection on each Sunday in order to allow you to rest, reflect, and rejoice. When Sunday comes each week, feast on these great truths with much joy and celebration in your heart.

A word about fasting: Traditionally, Lent is a time when we fast, or give things up. When we deny ourselves familiar comforts, we learn something powerful about our weaknesses, our needs, and our deepest longing for God. Fasting is a tangible, physical activity that points to our spiritual longing to be rooted in Jesus alone and find our true comfort and joy in him. Fasting is not essential to observing Lent, and certainly not essential to our life in Christ. We have received Christ Jesus through faith alone in him, and we walk in Christ in the same way. However, as Dallas Willard so wisely said, "Grace is not opposed to effort, it is opposed to earning."[1] Our own personal encouragement to you then, not from the Lord, is to consider how you might meaningfully engage in the discipline of fasting this Lenten season as a means of further soaking in the grace of God.

Lastly, our God is "able to do far more abundantly than all that we ask or think, according to the power at work within us" (Ephesians 3:20). Give

---

[1] Dallas Willard, *The Great Omission: Reclaiming Jesus's Essential Teachings on Discipleship* (San Francisco, CA: HarperSanFrancisco, 2006), 34.

yourself to him this Lenten season through meditation, preparation, and repentance. Your reward will be the same as that of Jesus: the overwhelming joy of Easter resurrection. May you be renewed in your love and affection for him!

THE FIRST DAYS OF LENT

Day 1: Ash Wednesday

Daily Readings

CALL TO WORSHIP

Blow a trumpet in Zion; sound an alarm on my holy mountain! Let all the inhabitants of the land tremble, for the day of the LORD is coming; it is near, a day of darkness and gloom, a day of clouds and thick darkness! Like blackness there is spread upon the mountains a great and powerful people; their like has never been before, nor will be again after them through the years of all generations. "Yet even now," declares the LORD, "return to me with all your heart, with fasting, with weeping, and with mourning; and rend your hearts and not your garments." Return to the LORD your God, for he is gracious and merciful, slow to anger, and abounding in steadfast love; and he relents over disaster.

Joel 2:1–2, 12–13

CONFESSION

Have mercy on me, O God, according to your unfailing love; according to your great compassion blot out my transgressions. Wash away all my iniquity and cleanse me from my sin. Surely you desire truth in the inner parts; you teach me wisdom in the inmost place. Create in me a pure heart, O God, and renew a steadfast spirit within me. Do not cast me from your presence or take your Holy Spirit from me. Restore to me the joy of your salvation and grant me a willing spirit, to sustain me. Amen.

Psalm 51:1–2, 6, 10–12

GOSPEL OF MARK

And Jesus went on with his disciples to the villages of Caesarea Philippi. And on the way he asked his disciples, "Who do people say that I am?" And they told him, "John the Baptist; and others say, Elijah; and others, one of the prophets." And he asked them, "But who do you say that I am?" Peter answered him, "You are the Christ." And he strictly charged them to tell no one about him.

Mark 8:27–30

PRAYER OF THANKSGIVING

Father God, in your steadfast love and mercy you have not despised the broken and contrite heart. Christ Jesus, you have borne our sins in your body on the tree and healed us by your wounds. Holy Spirit, you have led us into truth and spoken words of pardon and peace. Thanks be to our gracious and merciful Triune God.

Daily Devotion

Now if we have died with Christ, we believe that we will also live with him. We know that Christ, being raised from the dead, will never die again; death no longer has dominion over him. For the death he died he died to sin, once for all, but the life he lives he lives to God. So you also must consider yourselves dead to sin and alive to God in Christ Jesus.

Romans 6:8–11

Ash Wednesday marks the beginning of the Lenten season. The aim of Ash Wednesday is threefold: to meditate on our need for a Savior; to renew our commitment to daily repentance; and to remember with confidence and gratitude that Jesus has conquered sin and death. Our worship today should be filled with dependence and hope in Christ because of the power of our union with him and to the daily dying and rising with Christ that comes with this unity.

During a traditional Ash Wednesday service, ashes are applied to the worshiper's forehead (the "imposition") in the shape of a cross. In Scripture ashes or dust symbolize mortality (Genesis 18:27), mourning (Esther 4:3), judgment (Lamentations 3:16), and repentance (John 3:6).

An ashen cross serves as a reminder that you come from dust and to dust you shall return one day. It is also a call to "consider yourselves dead to sin and alive to God in Christ Jesus" (Romans 6:11).

As you begin this journey of Lent, you must start with rending your heart—tearing it from self-absorption and binding yourself (mind and devotion) to Jesus. Regardless of your current state or your proneness to wander, heed the call of the prophet Joel: "Return to the LORD your God, for he is gracious and merciful, slow to anger, and abounding in steadfast love" (Joel 2:13). After all, Lent is not about your faithfulness, but rather about the faithfulness of Jesus on your behalf. He is the faithful One!

REFLECTION QUESTIONS

1. Spend some time being still before God, asking the Spirit to search you: "Search me, O God, and know my heart! Try me and know my thoughts! And see if there be any grievous way in me, and lead me in the way everlasting!" (Psalm 139:23–24).
2. What hesitations or hindrances do you have in beginning this journey of Lent?
3. What habits and/or tendencies of self-absorption do you need to tear yourself from?

CLOSING PRAYER

Journey with us, O holy God, as we begin our way to the cross. Sharpen our focus, that our attention may center more on you than ourselves. Lead us through the shadows of darkness and prepare our hearts, that we might be a people of prayer, ready to perceive and respond to your Son and our Savior, Jesus Christ. In his name we pray. Amen.[1]

---

[1] *The Worship Sourcebook* (Grand Rapids, MI: Calvin Institute of Christian Worship, 2004), 557.

Day 2

Daily Readings

CALL TO WORSHIP

> The LORD upholds all who are falling and raises up all who are bowed down. The eyes of all look to you, and you give them their food in due season. You open your hand; you satisfy the desire of every living thing. The LORD is righteous in all his ways and kind in all his works. The LORD is near to all who call on him, to all who call on him in truth. He fulfills the desire of those who fear him; he also hears their cry and saves them. The LORD preserves all who love him, but all the wicked he will destroy. My mouth will speak the praise of the LORD, and let all flesh bless his holy name forever and ever.
>
> Psalm 145:14–21

CONFESSION

Holy and merciful Father, we confess to you . . . that we have sinned by our own fault in thought, word, and deed; by what we have done and by what we have left undone. We have not loved you with our whole heart, and mind, and strength. We have not loved our neighbors as ourselves. We have not forgiven others as we have been forgiven. We have been deaf to your call to serve, as Christ served us . . . We have grieved your Holy Spirit.[2]

GOSPEL OF MARK

> And he began to teach them that the Son of Man must suffer many things and be rejected by the elders and the chief priests and the

---

[2] *The Book of Common Prayer* (New York: Church Hymnal, 1979), 267.

scribes and be killed, and after three days rise again. And he said this plainly. And Peter took him aside and began to rebuke him. But turning and seeing his disciples, he rebuked Peter and said, "Get behind me, Satan! For you are not setting your mind on the things of God, but on the things of man." And calling the crowd to him with his disciples, he said to them, "If anyone would come after me, let him deny himself and take up his cross and follow me. For whoever would save his life will lose it, but whoever loses his life for my sake and the gospel's will save it. For what does it profit a man to gain the whole world and forfeit his soul? For what can a man give in return for his soul? For whoever is ashamed of me and of my words in this adulterous and sinful generation, of him will the Son of Man also be ashamed when he comes in the glory of his Father with the holy angels."

Mark 8:31–38

PRAYER OF THANKSGIVING

Lord Jesus, in submitting yourself to your Father's will, you denied yourself, laid down your life, and took up death on a cross. You willingly gave up your life to save ours. All praise and blessing be to your holy name.

Daily Devotion

And when you fast, do not look gloomy like the hypocrites, for they disfigure their faces that their fasting may be seen by others. Truly, I say to you, they have received their reward. But when you fast, anoint your head and wash your face, that your fasting may not be seen by others but by your Father who is in secret. And your Father who sees in secret will reward you.

Matthew 6:16–18

You may be familiar with the outward aspects of Lent: ashes on foreheads, conversation about giving up some kind of food or technology. But Lent, like spiritual life in general, is not merely external. There are internal realities that give depth and meaning to our actions; things like humility, sacrifice, repentance, and faith.

Jesus warned against focusing on wanting others to praise you for your acts of worship. He doesn't mean that it's wrong for people to see our actions. In fact, in the previous chapter, Jesus said, "let your light shine before others, so that they may see your good works and give glory to your Father who is in heaven" (Matthew 5:16). Jesus's point is that whatever we do should shine with the glory of God and be giving glory to God.

So if we are giving up caffeine, for example, we are doing it as a means of focusing our attention on God. We will be tempted to make it a measure of our devotion and maturity, but that is precisely the kind of thing Jesus criticizes in Matthew 6. If your focus were on giving up coffee for forty days, then you would be depriving yourself of far more than coffee. You would miss something that God wants to do in you during this season.

Jesus fasted from food and water for forty days in the wilderness. It was not a religious ritual or even a display of his self-control. Rather, it was a time of trial and temptation which he endured by entrusting himself to God and being nourished on the Word of God. The point of the wilderness, for Jesus, was to experience the real presence of God with him, and power of God at work in him.

The Lenten practice of denying ourselves usual comforts is a means of deepening our sense of union with Jesus, and reorienting our life around the things of God. We give up that which distracts and entangles because we want to experience our joy and freedom in Christ.

The Bible talks about fasting, but it does not prescribe a specific practice of fasting. Giving something up for Lent is not an issue of Christian obedience. The real goal is to feast on Jesus, and for some, a period of self-denial can whet the appetite in good and godly ways.

If you are considering what to give up for Lent, begin with whatever habits or things lie at the heart of your consumer lifestyle. What do you run to for comfort and pleasure and entertainment? What, if you didn't have it, would be a persistent reminder to run to Jesus?

Lent is not about what we do for Christ. It is about plumbing the depths of what he has done for us. It can be a deeply meaningful journey so long as we are focused on Jesus and dependent on the Holy Spirit. The journey is not made by willpower, but by faith.

REFLECTION QUESTIONS

1. Think about your day, your week. What activities consume the most of your time and attention?
2. Which of these activities might you give up for a time so that you could focus on your relationship with Jesus?
3. In what ways do you sense a need for the Spirit of God to make Jesus real to you?

CLOSING PRAYER

Lord, you have been our dwelling place in all generations. Before the mountains were brought forth, or you had formed the earth and the world, from everlasting to everlasting you are God. Teach us, Lord, to count our days that we may gain a wise heart. Satisfy us in the morning with your steadfast love, so that we may rejoice and be glad all our days. Through Christ, our Lord. Amen.[3]

---

[3] *The Worship Sourcebook*, 543.

Day 3

Daily Readings

CALL TO WORSHIP

A voice cries: "In the wilderness prepare the way of the LORD; make straight in the desert a highway for our God. Every valley shall be lifted up, and every mountain and hill be made low; the uneven ground shall become level, and the rough places a plain. And the glory of the LORD shall be revealed, and all flesh shall see it together, for the mouth of the LORD has spoken." A voice says, "Cry!" And I said, "What shall I cry?" All flesh is grass, and all its beauty is like the flower of the field. The grass withers, the flower fades when the breath of the LORD blows on it; surely the people are grass. The grass withers, the flower fades, but the word of our God will stand forever.

Isaiah 40:3–8

CONFESSION

Almighty God, we enter your presence humbly, aware that we approach you from a world that chooses to walk in darkness, apart from you. Each one of us has ignored and even denied the enlightening power of Jesus Christ. We confess now our sins to you, God of power and might. Penetrate our darkness by the power of Christ's light, that we may live in the joy of knowing and loving you and each other. We pray through Jesus Christ, our Lord. Amen.[4]

---

[4] *The Worship Sourcebook*, 535.

GOSPEL OF MARK

And he said to them, "Truly, I say to you, there are some standing here who will not taste death until they see the kingdom of God after it has come with power." And after six days Jesus took with him Peter and James and John, and led them up a high mountain by themselves. <u>And he was transfigured before them</u>, and his clothes <u>became radiant, intensely white, as no one on earth could bleach them.</u> And there appeared to them <u>Elijah with Moses</u>, and they were talking with Jesus. And Peter said to Jesus, "Rabbi, it is good that we are here. Let us make three tents, one for you and one for Moses and one for Elijah." For he did not know what to say, for they were terrified. And a cloud overshadowed them, and a voice came out of the cloud, "<u>This is my beloved Son; listen to him.</u>" And suddenly, looking around, they no longer saw anyone with them but Jesus only.

Mark 9:1–8

PRAYER OF THANKSGIVING

Eternal God, you have straightened our paths and made a way for us. You have illumined us with the light of Christ, in whose face we see your glory. In Jesus Christ we are forgiven and transformed! Thanks be to God!

Daily Devotion

But, as it is written, "What no eye has seen, nor ear heard, nor the heart of man imagined, what God has prepared for those who love him"— these things God has revealed to us through the Spirit. For the Spirit searches everything, even the depths of God.

1 Corinthians 2:9–10

At the onset of Jesus's ministry, John announced his coming in fulfillment of Isaiah 40: "In the wilderness prepare the way of the LORD; make straight in the desert a highway for our God." This is also the cry of Lent: Prepare the way of the Lord! Make room for him in your thoughts and activities and affections.

An <u>appropriate response</u> to this announcement is to <u>take stock of our lives, to reconsider</u> how we are living in light of God's presence and power made available to us in Jesus. That is what Lent is for—to reflect on our lives as they are and as they could be.

But take note: we could never imagine "what God has prepared for those who love him . . . for the Spirit searches everything, even the depths of God" (1 Corinthians 2:9–10). In every step of this journey, we yield to the Spirit's leading and power.

Giving up a habit or a food or a pleasure is not distinctly Christian. People give up things all the time in the name of self-help, or worse, vanity and even vengeance. The point of Lent is to reorient life God-ward. This reorientation has to do with desert and wilderness.

A "wilderness experience" in our language usually means one has been gone for a while and now returns with new insight or perspective, "a new lease on life." Whether it is a trip to the third world, or a hike in the mountains, people are stripped of their usual comforts, removed from the safety of familiarity, and are forced to see the world from a different vantage point.

Our aim during Lent is something like a wilderness experience. We want to shake up our lives significantly enough that when we reach for our usual comforts and grasp a fistful of air, we are forced to cling to Christ—his body, his blood. We want to see just how upside down our world really is as our "important things" prove to be perishable goods, and as our "busy" lives are shown to simply lack wisdom.

The point of giving things up is not to be reminded of how much we miss them, but rather to be awakened to how much we miss God and long for his life-giving Spirit. This means, of course, that Lent is not only about giving up things. It is also about adding things, God-things.

>> *Having given up junk food for a healthy diet, what will you do with the energy you gain?*

>> *Having given up internet surfing, what will you read now?*

>> *Having given up lunch, how will you rely on God for the strength of "food from heaven"?*

> » *Having given up TV as a default activity, how will you use that time to cultivate quality time with friends and family?*
>
> » *Having given up isolation, how will you immerse yourself in community?*
>
> » *Having given up shopping, how will you reach out to share what you have with people in your community?*

Don't worry about whether or not your sacrifice is a good one. It's not a contest. Just make your aim to know Christ more fully, and trust him to lead you. Seek to replace that thing with devotion to Christ—his Word and his mission. God may lead you to give up and take up more as you go. That's good. Deny yourself, take up your cross and follow Jesus.

REFLECTION QUESTIONS

1. Is the Lord leading you to give something up for Lent? If so, what?
2. Is God leading you to add something during this season? If so, what?

CLOSING PRAYER

Merciful God, we come to you today realizing that we are not how you want us to be. Help us let go of our past, that we may turn toward you and live again the life of faith. Help us call out our fear and hatred, our anger and self-pity. Lift the burden they place on our shoulders. Help us set aside our guilt and enter a season of healing. As we pray and fast today, help us become simple people, that we may see you plainly. Let us draw near to you now. Amen.[5]

---

[5] *The Worship Sourcebook*, 544.

Day 4

Daily Readings

CALL TO WORSHIP

> Therefore, since we are surrounded by so great a cloud of witnesses, let us also lay aside every weight, and sin which clings so closely, and let us run with endurance the race that is set before us, looking to Jesus, the founder and perfecter of our faith, who for the joy that was set before him endured the cross, despising the shame, and is seated at the right hand of the throne of God. Consider him who endured from sinners such hostility against himself, so that you may not grow weary or fainthearted.
>
> Hebrews 12:1–3

CONFESSION

Father of mercies, we confess that we have sinned against you. By your Holy Spirit, come and work repentance into our hearts. Help us to see you as you are: with outstretched arms, a loving heart, and power to save. Help us to see Jesus, the friend of sinners, and to follow him more faithfully. As we have received him, so strengthen us to walk in him, depend on him, commune with him, and be conformed to him. Give us an experience of your grace that makes us bold, that we might joyfully live for the good of others. Amen.

GOSPEL OF MARK

> And as they were coming down the mountain, he charged them to tell no one what they had seen, until the Son of Man had risen from the dead. So they kept the matter to themselves, questioning

what this rising from the dead might mean. And they asked him, "Why do the scribes say that first Elijah must come?" And he said to them, "Elijah does come first to restore all things. And how is it written of the Son of Man that he should suffer many things and be treated with contempt? But I tell you that Elijah has come, and they did to him whatever they pleased, as it is written of him."

Mark 9:9–13

PRAYER OF THANKSGIVING

Lord Jesus, we turn our eyes to you: who endured the cross, who despised the shame, who suffered many things, and who is now seated at the right hand of the throne of God. You are the founder and perfecter of our faith!

Daily Devotion

There is therefore now no condemnation for those who are in Christ Jesus. For the law of the Spirit of life has set you free in Christ Jesus from the law of sin and death. For God has done what the law, weakened by the flesh, could not do. By sending his own Son in the likeness of sinful flesh and for sin, he condemned sin in the flesh, in order that the righteous requirement of the law might be fulfilled in us, who walk not according to the flesh but according to the Spirit.

Romans 8:1–4

Lent is a journey that ends with resurrection, but by way of the desert and the cross. Anyone who takes it seriously quickly discovers the challenge of entering into this wilderness. It is not a casual shift—we must devote ourselves to it as a matter of the heart. Nor is it a sudden shift—we have to unravel our entangled habits and settle down our preoccupied minds. In these first few days, we have been trying to downshift slowly and thoughtfully from our normal routine into the rhythms of Lent.

There are perhaps a few groups of people at this point: latecomers, early goers, and those who are neither here nor there.

Latecomers: If Lent were a party, you just walked in the door and aren't quite sure what has already been said and done. Part of you wants to blend in like you know what you are doing, and part of you wonders if you should just go home and try to make it on time next year. Good news for you: The Lent party is a gospel party! The gospel of Jesus does not discriminate against when or how you got here. It only beckons you to come as you are.

What should you do now that you are here? Set aside some time for understanding and prayer. Catch up on the readings, worship Jesus, and ask him to lead you in this journey. Decide on something that you will give up and something that you will take up in order to draw near to God. Or, perhaps God is not leading you to give anything up, but simply to focus your attention on him. Do not worry about what you have missed or whether or not you are doing it right. "Seek first the kingdom of God and his righteousness, and all these things will be added to you" (Matthew 6:33).

Early Goers: If Lent were a race, you are starting to lose energy. You began with enthusiasm, but you have already forgotten at times what you are supposed to be doing, or you may simply feel defeated by how well everyone else seems to be doing. Good news for you: You are worse than you think, but also far more loved by God than you ever imagined.[6] There is no condemnation for those who are in Christ Jesus (Romans 8:1), which means you have been set free from "performing Lent." Indeed, the very thing that Lent beckons us to consider is Jesus, who on the cross took the blow for all of our unfaithfulness and shame once for all, so that we may breathe easy in the company of God's family.

What should you do if you have already strayed? Get back on course. Repent of making Lent about what you do or don't do (or what other people do) and run to the cross where "God has done what the law, weakened by the flesh, could not do . . . by sending his own Son in the likeness of sinful flesh" (Romans 8:3).

Neither Here nor There: You are neither here (late) nor there (gone). You are running with the pack, fully present at the party. Good news for you: The gospel is deeper and fuller than you ever imagined! "Run the race that is set before us, looking to Jesus" (Hebrews 12:1–2).

---

[6] Quoted in *Saving Grace: Devotions from Jack Miller*, (Greensboro, NC: New Growth Press, 2014), xv.

This is what Lent is about: joining the company of God's people to consider Jesus's suffering and death; denying ourselves and being sustained by God so that we may run straighter and stronger; gaining hope and strength from the faithfulness of God in Christ Jesus. Wherever you are today—behind, astray, on course—fix your eyes on Jesus, our brave frontrunner and generous host.

REFLECTION QUESTIONS

1. What have you learned about God and yourself in these first days of Lent?
2. What areas of fear or pride are hindering you from fully committing to this journey?
3. Write down one area in your life where you can clearly see your need for the forgiveness Jesus provided at the cross. Then write down one area in your life where you are weak and need the power of the Holy Spirit to help you.

CLOSING PRAYER

O Lord our God, long-suffering and full of compassion: Be present with us as we enter this season in which we recall our Savior's sufferings and celebrate his triumph. Give us your Holy Spirit, so that as we acknowledge our sins and implore your pardon, we may also have the strength to deny ourselves and be upheld in times of temptation through Jesus Christ, our Lord. Amen.[1]

---

[1] *The Worship Sourcebook*, 544.

FIRST SUNDAY OF LENT

This is the good news that we have received, in which we stand, and by which we are saved: Christ died for our sins, was buried, was raised on the third day, and appeared first to the women, then to Peter and the Twelve, and then to many faithful witnesses. We believe Jesus is the Christ, the Anointed One of God, the firstborn of all creation, the firstborn from the dead, in whom all things hold together, in whom the fullness of God was pleased to dwell by the power of the Spirit. Christ is the head of the body, the church, and by the blood of the cross reconciles all things to God. Amen.[2]

> Low in the grave He lay,
> Jesus, my Savior,
> Waiting the coming day,
> Jesus, my Lord!
>
> Up from the grave He arose,
> With a mighty triumph o'er His foes,
> He arose a Victor from the dark domain,
> And He lives forever, with His saints to reign.
> He arose! He arose!
> Hallelujah! Christ arose!
>
> Vainly they watch His bed,
> Jesus, my Savior;
> Vainly they seal the dead,
> Jesus, my Lord!
>
> Death cannot keep his prey,
> Jesus, my Savior;
> He tore the bars away,
> Jesus, my Lord![3]

---

[2] Adapted from 1 Corinthians 15 and Colossians 1
[3] Robert Lowry, "Up from the Grave He Arose", 1874.

WEEK ONE: REPENTANCE

Day 5

Daily Readings

CALL TO WORSHIP

Bless the LORD, O my soul, and all that is within me, bless his holy name! Bless the LORD, O my soul, and forget not all his benefits, who forgives all your iniquity, who heals all your diseases, who redeems your life from the pit, who crowns you with steadfast love and mercy, who satisfies you with good so that your youth is renewed like the eagle's.

Psalm 103:1–5

CONFESSION

Father in heaven, we need to be forgiven. Instead of trusting in the death of Jesus Christ, we have trusted in our own merit. We have tried so hard to pile up good deeds that outweigh our sins. Instead of trusting in the resurrection of Jesus Christ, we have tried to change through our own efforts. We have tried to change our hearts through sheer willpower. Forgive us for neglecting your grace. Forgive us and heal us, for Jesus's sake. Amen.

GOSPEL OF MARK

And when they came to the disciples, they saw a great crowd around them, and scribes arguing with them. And immediately all the crowd, when they saw him, were greatly amazed and ran up to him and greeted him. And he asked them, "What are you arguing about with them?" And someone from the crowd answered him, "Teacher, I brought my son to you, for he has a spirit that makes him mute.

And whenever it seizes him, it throws him down, and he foams and grinds his teeth and becomes rigid. So I asked your disciples to cast it out, and they were not able." And he answered them, "O faithless generation, how long am I to be with you? How long am I to bear with you? <u>Bring him to me</u>." And they brought the boy to him. And when the spirit saw him, immediately it convulsed the boy, and he fell on the ground and rolled about, foaming at the mouth. And Jesus asked his father, "How long has this been happening to him?" And he said, "From childhood. And it has often cast him into fire and into water, to destroy him. But if you can do anything, have compassion on us and help us." And Jesus said to him, "'If you can'! All things are possible for one who believes." Immediately the father of the child cried out and said, "<u>I believe; help my unbelief</u>!" And when Jesus saw that a crowd came running together, he rebuked the unclean spirit, saying to it, "You mute and deaf spirit, <u>I command you, come out of him and never enter him again</u>." And after crying out and convulsing him terribly, it came out, and the boy was like a corpse, so that most of them said, "He is dead." But Jesus took him by the hand and lifted him up, and he arose. And when he had entered the house, his disciples asked him privately, "Why could we not cast it out?" And he said to them, "Thi<u>s kind cannot be driven out by anything but prayer</u>."

Mark 9:14–29

PRAYER OF THANKSGIVING

God of mercy, in Christ you have forgiven all our iniquity, healed and made us whole, redeemed our life from the pit, and poured out your love and goodness upon us. My soul blesses the Lord!

Daily Devotion

Return to the LORD your God, for he is gracious and merciful, slow to anger, and abounding in steadfast love.

Joel 2:13

Lent is a time of particular focus on repentance, which does not mean that we atone for our sins, or even that we feel deep shame about them. Repentance is taking a different course in light of the fact that Jesus atoned for our sins and bore our shame on the cross.

JOURNEY TO THE CROSS

The word "repentance" often has a negative connotation. To say that someone needs to repent implies they have done something really bad, and should feel really bad about it. While that may be true in some respect, the call to repentance is fundamentally good news. One Bible commentator says, "Repentance from the beginning of time to this present hour has been, and remains, the most positive Word from the heart of God."[4]

God made us for himself, but we are all prone to wander. Repentance is an invitation to come home, to turn to God and find rest and life in him.

The term used extensively by the Prophets (*shubh*) means "to turn" or "return," so the idea of returning from exile is in view. In the Old Testament, God disciplined his people by giving them over to captivity in pagan nations. It was horrific at every level: physical, cultural, and spiritual devastation. As awful as it sounds, it was actually a demonstration of God's love. As a father disciplines his children, "the Lord disciplines the one he loves, and chastises every son whom he receives" (Hebrews 12:6). The point of discipline is correction and restoration. It is an invitation to fellowship.

The apostle Paul says it is God's kindness that leads us to repentance (Romans 2:4). God calls us to himself, convicts us of our sins, comforts us with his love, and changes us by his grace. Our repentance begins and ends with God! When we make it about what we will do to make things right with God, we veer off the road of faith into one of two ditches.

On one side of the road, we express resolve: "I will never do that again!" We act as if we can wipe the slate clean with our sincerity and earn a pardon with our passion. When we promise to "never do that again," we are saying that we really can be good enough, and we'll prove it this time. But repentance is not a do-over. Nor is it a system of self-improvement. Turning to God means admitting that our way is not good, and our effort is not enough. God shows us a new way in Jesus, and gives us a new power by his Spirit. Faith in Jesus and reliance upon the Holy Spirit is how we "bear fruit in keeping with repentance" (Matthew 3:8).

---

[4] Richard Owen Roberts, *Repentance: The First Word of the Gospel*, (Wheaton, IL: Crossway, 2002).

On the other side of the road, we express remorse: "I can't believe I did that." Feelings of shame and guilt are natural, but the Bible says there are two kinds of grief for our sins: worldly and godly (2 Corinthians 7:10). "Worldly grief" turns us in on self so that we are primarily concerned with our feelings and self-interests. So we feel bad, but only because we got caught. We are troubled, but only until the negative attention goes away. A common symptom of worldly grief is self-loathing: If we can just feel bad enough, or punish ourselves enough, we can make up for what we've done and appease God's wrath against our sin.

"Godly grief," on the other hand, "produces a repentance that leads to salvation without regret" (2 Corinthians 7:10). When we experience godly grief, we understand that our sin is against God as well as others, and that it reflects a heart that naturally drifts (and runs!) from God. True repentance always sends us to Jesus. An honest sense of our sinfulness drives us toward the depth of Christ's mercy in the gospel.

Repentance is not how we get to God. It is our response to the good news that God has come to us in Christ.

REFLECTION QUESTIONS

1. In what areas are you trying to deal with sin through resolve or remorse?
2. Take a few moments and confess these things to God. Thank him for his grace and mercy in the gospel, and ask for the power of his Spirit to walk by faith.

CLOSING PRAYER

Gracious God, out of your love and mercy you breathed into dust the breath of life, creating us to serve you and our neighbors. In this season of repentance, restore to us the joy of our salvation and strengthen us to face our mortality, that we may reach with confidence for your mercy, in Jesus Christ, our Lord, who lives and reigns with you and the Holy Spirit, one God, now and forever. Amen.[5]

---

[5] *The Worship Sourcebook*, 548.

Day 6

Daily Readings

CALL TO WORSHIP

I will recount the steadfast love of the LORD, the praises of the
LORD, according to all that the LORD has granted us, and the great
goodness to the house of Israel that he has granted them according
to his compassion, according to the abundance of his steadfast love.
For he said, "Surely they are my people, children who will not deal
falsely." And he became their Savior. In all their affliction he was
afflicted, and the angel of his presence saved them; in his love and
in his pity he redeemed them; he lifted them up and carried them
all the days of old.

Isaiah 63:7–9

CONFESSION

Our Father, forgive us for thinking small thoughts of you and for
ignoring your immensity and greatness. Lord Jesus, forgive us for
forgetting that you rule the nations and our small lives. Holy Spirit,
forgive us for quenching your power and squandering your gifts. We
confess that our blindness to your glory, O triune God, has resulted in
shallow confession, tepid conviction, and only mild repentance. Have
mercy upon us in the name of the Father, the Son, and the Holy Spirit.
Amen.[6]

---

[6] *The Worship Sourcebook*, 102.

GOSPEL OF MARK

They went on from there and passed through Galilee. And he did not want anyone to know, for he was teaching his disciples, saying to them, "The Son of Man is going to be delivered into the hands of men, and they will kill him. And when he is killed, after three days he will rise." But they did not understand the saying, and were afraid to ask him. And they came to Capernaum. And when he was in the house he asked them, "What were you discussing on the way?" But they kept silent, for on the way they had argued with one another about who was the greatest. And he sat down and called the twelve. And he said to them, "If anyone would be first, he must be last of all and servant of all." And he took a child and put him in the midst of them, and taking him in his arms, he said to them, "Whoever receives one such child in my name receives me, and whoever receives me, receives not me but him who sent me."

Mark 9:30–37

PRAYER OF THANKSGIVING

We boast in your greatness, Father God, and in the greatness of your Son, Jesus Christ. He made himself nothing in order to serve us. He was afflicted in order to redeem us. He was cut off from you so that we might be joined as your people. All glory be to Christ!

Daily Devotion

"Yet even now," declares the LORD, "return to me with all your heart, with fasting, with weeping, and with mourning; and rend your hearts and not your garments."

Joel 2:12–13a

Last Wednesday, people around the world marked their foreheads with ash as a sign of their humanity and mortality. We find this symbolism and practice throughout the Bible. When Abraham petitioned God, he said, "Behold, I have undertaken to speak to the Lord, I who am but dust and ashes" (Genesis 18:27). When the people of Nineveh heeded Jonah's warning, the king "arose from his throne, removed his robe, covered himself with sackcloth, and sat in ashes" (Jonah 3:6). This is the posture of repentance.

In the Old Testament, when God's people went astray, there was often a corporate aspect to their repentance. They would fast and mourn and pray together for God to heal and bless their nation. That kind of repentance is appropriate when we find ourselves feeling the consequences of cultural or national sin. For instance, I am both troubled and tempted by the rampant materialism and greed in our country. I am a participant, but it is much bigger than any one person. We need to repent corporately for these kinds of things.

As necessary as corporate repentance was and is, it can also become more about ritual than relationship. The prophets spoke out against this kind of empty worship. The prophet Joel warned Israel to "rend your hearts and not your garments" (Joel 2:13). The custom at the time was to tear their clothes as a sign of their grief. It was meant to be a reflection of their hearts and minds, but that wasn't always the case. It's always possible to go through the motions, to act outwardly as if you are troubled and grieved, but inwardly to remain unchanged.

What is the change that God is looking for? It is primarily a change in our worship. When we wander from God, it is because something else has captured our attention and affections. We have fallen in love with other gods. To "rend your heart" means tear yourself away from false lovers and return to your first love. Repentance is a deep feeling of grief that causes us to return to God and to worship him above all else.

The posture of repentance is to acknowledge our humanity before God, and to grieve our wayward hearts. But even in this low place, we do not hang our heads as those who cannot see past our failures. We lift our eyes to Jesus. Scottish pastor Robert Murray McCheyne said it this way: "For every look at yourself, take ten looks at Christ."[7]

John the Baptist was cut from the same fabric as the prophets. He called his own generation to make a radical turn in the direction of their lives by pointing them to Jesus: "Behold the lamb of God!" (John 1:36). Here is the beginning of repentance: turn your attention to Jesus. This is simple, but essential. "All things were created through him and for

---

[7] *Memoir and Remains of the Rev. Robert Murray McCheyne* (Edinburgh, 1894), 293.

him" (Colossians 1:16), so any form of repentance involves looking to Jesus, "full of grace and truth" (John 1:14).

In Christ, our ashes are turned to beauty, for he has clothed us with the garments of salvation and covered us with the robes of righteousness (Isaiah 61:10).

REFLECTION QUESTIONS

1. What areas of your life seem apart from God's control? Where is it difficult to feel God's presence in your circumstances?
2. Is there any area of your life in which you are resistant to God's control? Confess this in prayer to him.

CLOSING PRAYER

God of love, as in Jesus Christ you gave yourself to us, so may we give ourselves to you, living according to your holy will. Keep our feet firmly in the way where Christ leads us; make our mouths speak the truth that Christ teaches us; fill our bodies with the life that is Christ within us. In his holy name we pray. Amen.[8]

---

[8] *The Worship Sourcebook*, 578.

Day 7

Daily Readings

CALL TO WORSHIP

In the beginning was the Word, and the Word was with God, and the Word was God. He was in the beginning with God. All things were made through him, and without him was not any thing made that was made. In him was life, and the life was the light of men. The light shines in the darkness, and the darkness has not overcome it.

John 1:1–5

CONFESSION

Almighty and merciful God, we confess that we have sinned against you and one another in both our actions and our inactions. We recognize that in Jesus Christ our light has come, yet often we choose to walk in shadows and ignore the light. Gracious God, forgive our sins and remove from us the veil of darkness that shrouds our lives. Illumined by your Word and sacrament, may we rise to the radiance of Christ's glory. Amen.[9]

GOSPEL OF MARK

John said to him, "Teacher, we saw someone casting out demons in your name, and we tried to stop him, because he was not following us." But Jesus said, "Do not stop him, for no one who does a mighty work in my name will be able soon afterward to speak evil of me. For the one who is not against us is for us. For truly, I say to you, whoever gives you a cup of water to drink because you belong to Christ will by no means lose his reward. Whoever causes one of

---

[9] *The Worship Sourcebook*, 502.

these little ones who believe in me to sin, it would be better for him if a great millstone were hung around his neck and he were thrown into the sea. And if your hand causes you to sin, cut it off. It is better for you to enter life crippled than with two hands to go to hell, to the unquenchable fire. And if your foot causes you to sin, cut it off. It is better for you to enter life lame than with two feet to be thrown into hell. And if your eye causes you to sin, tear it out. It is better for you to enter the kingdom of God with one eye than with two eyes to be thrown into hell, 'where their worm does not die and the fire is not quenched.' For everyone will be salted with fire. Salt is good, but if the salt has lost its saltiness, how will you make it salty again? Have salt in yourselves, and be at peace with one another."

Mark 9:38–50

PRAYER OF THANKSGIVING

God, you are light, and in you there is no darkness at all. The light of your Son, Jesus, pierces our world and shines in our darkness. He cleanses us from all sin and restores our fellowship with you and with others. Praise be to God, the author of light!

Daily Devotion

How sweet are your words to my taste, sweeter than honey to my mouth! Through your precepts I get understanding; therefore I hate every false way. Your word is a lamp to my feet and a light to my path.

Psalm 119:103–105

An honest friend once confessed, "My struggle with repentance has to do with knowing myself well enough to see what I should repent of." Even when we know that repentance is important in general, sometimes we do not know what to repent of in particular. Similarly, sometimes we have a matter to bring to God, but we do not know the depths of it. This is why we begin by seeking the face of God, because we need the bright light of God's presence to shine into the dark corners of our soul.

This is the good news that John proclaims, "God is light, and in him is no darkness at all" (1 John 1:5). In the Old Testament, "light" speaks to the character of God and the truth of his Word. In John's writings, "light" is the glory of God revealed in his Word and in The Word that became flesh—the person of Christ. There is no falsehood in what he has revealed. It is right and trustworthy and pure.

To address God is to come into the light of truth. It is not a formality, but rather a desperate cry: "Search me, O God, and know my heart! Try me and know my thoughts! And see if there be any grievous way in me" (Psalm 139:23–24).

That God is the one who beckons and arouses our repentance is what makes it more than empty ritual. Resolve and remorse are aroused by fear and pride. Regarding fear, I turn from my ways because I dread consequence or loss of approval from others. Regarding pride, I tell myself that I need to turn from my ways because "I'm a good Christian. I must stop doing this because I don't want to be like 'those people.' I'm not like that."

You cannot fix or manage the problem of sin. You can only be rescued from it and sanctified in the midst of it.

If you are observing Lent—denying usual comforts, reorienting your life in some way around the things of God—then isn't this your prayer? God, illuminate my path! Search my heart and test my anxious thoughts. Shed light on my dark ways. I want a clear picture of what my life is about, and where it is headed. How will I turn from my ways if I cannot see them?

When we feel the pains of hunger, the habitual desire to watch TV, the consuming desire to buy something, our thoughts turn here: "Search me, O God." We want to know the ways that sin has entangled us, blinded us, distorted our tastes and weakened our desires. We are preparing the way in our heart for God to speak, making straight a path in our soul for the Spirit to work.

How does God search and test and illuminate? God has many instruments, I suppose, but we must begin with the sharpest one. The Bible is the Word of God, "sharper than any two-edged sword, piercing to the division of soul and of spirit . . . discerning the thoughts and intentions of the heart" (Hebrews 4:12). His Word searches us, convicts us, enlightens us, and leads us. This is why a greater devotion to the Bible is a good idea during the Lenten season. Remember, we give up and take up. When we give up something, we make a clearing in our lives, but unless the clearing is filled up with light, we still stumble around in the dark.

REFLECTION QUESTIONS

1. In what areas of your life are you merely trying to fix or manage the problem of sin?
2. What would it look like for you to move toward true repentance in that area?

CLOSING PRAYER

Creator of the heavens and earth, speak light into our immeasurable darkness. Expose the chaos of our steps and bring order to our lives. Light of the World, full of grace and truth, open up the kingdom of heaven to us. Tell us what you hear and see and give us your ears and eyes.

Day 8

Daily Readings

CALL TO WORSHIP

Oh give thanks to the LORD; call upon his name; make known his deeds among the peoples! Sing to him, sing praises to him; tell of all his wondrous works! Glory in his holy name; let the hearts of those who seek the LORD rejoice! Seek the LORD and his strength; seek his presence continually! Remember the wondrous works that he has done, his miracles and the judgments he uttered, O offspring of Israel his servant, children of Jacob, his chosen ones! Sing to the LORD, all the earth! Tell of his salvation from day to day. Declare his glory among the nations, his marvelous works among all the peoples! For great is the LORD, and greatly to be praised, and he is to be held in awe above all gods. For all the gods of the peoples are idols, but the LORD made the heavens.

1 Chronicles 16:8–13, 23–26

CONFESSION

Lord, bring new life where I am worn and tired; new love where I have turned hard-hearted; forgiveness where I feel hurt and where I have wounded; and the joy and freedom of your Holy Spirit where I am a prisoner of myself. Search me, O God, and know my heart; try me and know my thoughts. See if there is any wicked way in me, and lead me in the way everlasting.[10]

---

[10] *The Worship Sourcebook*, 637. And Psalm 139-23-24.

GOSPEL OF MARK

And he left there and went to the region of Judea and beyond the Jordan, and crowds gathered to him again. And again, as was his custom, he taught them. And Pharisees came up and in order to test him asked, "Is it lawful for a man to divorce his wife?" He answered them, "What did Moses command you?" They said, "Moses allowed a man to write a certificate of divorce and to send her away." And Jesus said to them, "Because of your hardness of heart he wrote you this commandment. But from the beginning of creation, 'God made them male and female.' 'Therefore a man shall leave his father and mother and hold fast to his wife, and the two shall become one flesh.' So they are no longer two but one flesh. What therefore God has joined together, let not man separate." And in the house the disciples asked him again about this matter. And he said to them, "Whoever divorces his wife and marries another commits adultery against her, and if she divorces her husband and marries another, she commits adultery."

Mark 10:1–12

PRAYER OF THANKSGIVING

Thank you God for piercing our hard hearts and forgiving our stubborn rebellion. You have chosen us and made us your own. We rejoice in you and in your salvation!

Daily Devotion

This is the message we have heard from him and proclaim to you, that God is light, and in him is no darkness at all. If we say we have fellowship with him while we walk in darkness, we lie and do not practice the truth. But if we walk in the light, as he is in the light, we have fellowship with one another, and the blood of Jesus his Son cleanses us from all sin. If we say we have no sin, we deceive ourselves, and the truth is not in us. If we confess our sins, he is faithful and just to forgive us our sins and to cleanse us from all unrighteousness.

1 John 1:5–9

A mentor of mine used to say, "Reality is your friend," to which someone once replied, "But sometimes your friends are ugly."

When we bring our lives into the light, they aren't as pretty as we thought they were. But that is the reality we must embrace. It truly is our friend because it points us to God, who "is faithful and just to forgive us our sins and to cleanse us from all unrighteousness" (1 John 1:9).

The primary means by which we walk in the light with God is the simple act of confession. Confession does not secure forgiveness, but rather facilitates the power of forgiveness and its cleansing effects in the life of the believer. The acting agent is the blood of Jesus, his sacrificial death on the cross (1 John 1:7). Jesus is willing and able to cleanse us and restore our relationships if we will just get the real us in the light.

To walk in darkness means to neglect or even deny the truth about God, or about ourselves. A toddler may close his eyes and believe that he cannot be seen, but only because he does not see. So it is with the one who walks in darkness. He thinks his way of seeing things is in fact reality, but nothing could be further from the truth. He will not be able to have fellowship with God or with others until he sees according to truth. In the realm of truth, he will be able to relate to God and others on the basis of what is real, and experience the cleansing power of Jesus's blood.

That sounds great "on paper," but when it comes to our actual lives, we are not always so eager to be honest. Instead, we deal with reality in other ways. We distract ourselves with the artificial lights of work, entertainment, and hobbies. When ordinary busyness doesn't work, we take it up a notch and give ourselves to something so completely that it consumes us. These are our addictions. When we feel stressed or bored or frustrated or empty inside, they take us to another world where we can forget all our troubles, at least for a little while. Addictions are dangerous because we are not only ignoring reality, but also making it far worse.

Pretense, excuses, busyness, addiction, and despair are not our friends. They turn us in upon ourselves, which leads to death. An honest look at reality, with God's help, gives us insight into the way sin works and how God can bring healing and transformation to those areas of our lives. We can only repent of what we are able to see.

This is why community is such an essential context for true repentance. Our friends and family can see our blind spots, and we need them to tell us. We need a community where it is okay to talk about our struggle against temptation and sin, how sin is wrecking our lives, and how our brokenness causes us to look for worth and joy and peace outside of God. Can we talk about these things without condemning each other, or condoning sin? Can we talk about our problems without someone always fixing it with their "solutions"? Can we weep with those who weep, and pray for those who are struggling?

Search us, O God! Every dark corner and every hidden place. And knit us together in love (Colossians 2:2).

REFLECTION QUESTIONS

1. What is your practice of confession and repentance like? Where do you need to grow?
2. In what areas of your life are you guilty of walking in isolation? What areas of your life does no one know about? What areas of struggle do you need to invite your community into?

CLOSING PRAYER

God of transformation, God of the Lenten journey, help us to discern your still, small voice. Open us to change and growth, that we may walk with Christ. In Jesus's name, Amen.[11]

---

[11] *The Worship Sourcebook*, 570.

Day 9

Daily Readings

CALL TO WORSHIP

> For God alone, O my soul, wait in silence, for my hope is from him. He only is my rock and my salvation, my fortress; I shall not be shaken. On God rests my salvation and my glory; my mighty rock, my refuge is God. Trust in him at all times, O people; pour out your heart before him; God is a refuge for us.
>
> Psalm 62:5–8

CONFESSION

Everlasting God, fountain of all life and the true home of every heart: our hearts are restless until they rest in you. Yet we confess that our hearts have been enslaved by selfish passion and base desire. We have sought after many things and have neglected the one thing needful. We have not loved you with our whole hearts; help us to turn to you and find forgiveness. Lead us home, that we may again find in you our life and joy and peace. Amen.[12]

GOSPEL OF MARK

> And they were bringing children to him that he might touch them, and the disciples rebuked them. But when Jesus saw it, he was indignant and said to them, "Let the children come to me; do not hinder them, for to such belongs the kingdom of God. Truly, I say to you, whoever does not receive the kingdom of God like a child

---

[12] *The Worship Sourcebook*, 564.

shall not enter it." And he took them in his arms and blessed them, laying his hands on them.

Mark 10:13–16

PRAYER OF THANKSGIVING

We love and praise you, O God, for your abundant mercy and your wide embrace. You welcome us into your arms, and it is there that we find true rest and peace for our souls. Thanks be to God.

Daily Devotion

Whoever conceals his transgressions will not prosper, but he who confesses and forsakes them will obtain mercy.

Proverbs 28:13

Repentance begins with seeking God, embracing the way things really are by confessing them, and then turning from our wicked ways. For confession and turning to occur, we must take responsibility for our sin.

People commonly associate sin with specific actions that break God's rules. The biblical concept of sin is not less than that, but it is more, much more. Commenting on Soren Kierkegaard's book *The Sickness Unto Death*, Tim Keller says, "Sin is the despairing refusal to find your deepest identity in your relationship and service to God. Sin is seeking to become oneself, to get an identity, apart from God."[13]

We were made for God, to center our entire life on him and find our sense of worth and purpose in him. Anything other than that is sin. Keller continues: "Sin is not just the doing of bad things, but the making of good things into ultimate things. It is seeking to establish a sense of self by making something else more central to your significance, purpose, and happiness than your relationship with God."[14]

Israel's story is a cycle of running to other gods and then coming back to the Lord. We get caught in the same cycle, chasing after life apart from

---

[13] Timothy Keller, *The Reason for God: Belief in an Age of Skepticism* (London: Penguin Books, 2009), 162.
[14] Ibid.

God, and then running back to God in the aftermath of disappointment and disillusionment.

The gospel sets us free from this kind of fickle faith. God gives us a sure foundation in Christ by adopting us into his family, and sealing us with the Holy Spirit (Ephesians 1:5, 13). We don't need anything more than what we have been given in Christ. We cannot accomplish anything more than what he has already done on our behalf. Nothing can separate us from the love of God (Romans 8:39).

Therefore, we are free to accept responsibility for our sin without fear of condemnation (Romans 8:1). We not only admit that we have sinned, but also that we have sinned because we were tempted by our own desires, and willfully gave ourselves to them (James 1:14-15). This kind of ownership is necessary for true repentance, and stands in contrast to many of the ways we typically try to deal with our sin.

We try to justify our sin. When you become aware of sin, do you feel the need to nuance everything, explain how complicated things are, or make excuses? Taking responsibility for sin means we say, "I lusted because my desires are perverted" . . . "I lied because I am afraid of what people think about me" . . . "I ate that because I do not have self-control around food."

We try to downplay our sin, hoping that God overlooks it. We don't think sin really affects our ability to relate to God, or hinders the flow of his blessing. Taking responsibility for sin means we say, "My sin is destructive and grieves God. I need to deal with this."

We pretend things are better than they really are, cleaning the outside of the cup while we are still unclean on the inside. Taking responsibility means we say, "It doesn't matter how good people think I am. God sees right through me, and is not impressed or tricked by my lip service. God hates hypocrisy!"

Our problems are bigger than our circumstances: we are broken on the inside. And repentance is deeper than what we do: we need to repent of who we are. Conviction of sin is a difficult pill to swallow, but it is good medicine to the soul.

REFLECTION QUESTIONS

1. How have you been trying to build an identity apart from God?
2. How has that produced restlessness in your life?
3. What do you think it would mean to rest in God today?

CLOSING PRAYER

God of mercy, you are full of tenderness and compassion, slow to anger, rich in mercy, and always ready to forgive. Grant us grace to renounce all evil and to cling to Christ, that in every way we may prove to be your loving children, through Jesus Christ, our Lord, who lives and reigns with you and the Holy Spirit, one God, forever and ever. Amen.[15]

---

[15] *The Worship Sourcebook*, 577.

Day 10

Daily Readings

CALL TO WORSHIP

> For the love of Christ controls us, because we have concluded this: that one has died for all, therefore all have died; and he died for all, that those who live might no longer live for themselves but for him who for their sake died and was raised. From now on, therefore, we regard no one according to the flesh. Even though we once regarded Christ according to the flesh, we regard him thus no longer. Therefore, if anyone is in Christ, he is a new creation. The old has passed away; behold, the new has come. For our sake he made him to be sin who knew no sin, so that in him we might become the righteousness of God.
>
> 2 Corinthians 5:14–17, 21

CONFESSION

God of compassion, in Jesus Christ you did not disdain the company of sinners but welcomed them with love. Look upon us in mercy, we pray. Our sins are more than we can bear; our pasts enslave us; our misdeeds are beyond correcting. Forgive the wrongs we cannot undo; free us from a past we cannot change; heal what we can no longer fix. Grace our lives with your love and turn the tears of our past into the joys of new life with you. Amen.[16]

GOSPEL OF MARK

> And as he was setting out on his journey, a man ran up and knelt before him and asked him, "Good Teacher, what must I do to inherit

---

[16] *The Worship Sourcebook*, 564.

eternal life?" And Jesus said to him, "Why do you call me good? No one is good except God alone. You know the commandments: 'Do not murder, Do not commit adultery, Do not steal, Do not bear false witness, Do not defraud, Honor your father and mother.'" And he said to him, "Teacher, all these I have kept from my youth." And Jesus, looking at him, loved him, and said to him, "You lack one thing: go, sell all that you have and give to the poor, and you will have treasure in heaven; and come, follow me." Disheartened by the saying, he went away sorrowful, for he had great possessions. And Jesus looked around and said to his disciples, "How difficult it will be for those who have wealth to enter the kingdom of God!" And the disciples were amazed at his words. But Jesus said to them again, "Children, how difficult it is to enter the kingdom of God! It is easier for a camel to go through the eye of a needle than for a rich person to enter the kingdom of God." And they were exceedingly astonished, and said to him, "Then who can be saved?" Jesus looked at them and said, "With man it is impossible, but not with God. For all things are possible with God." Peter began to say to him, "See, we have left everything and followed you." Jesus said, "Truly, I say to you, there is no one who has left house or brothers or sisters or mother or father or children or lands, for my sake and for the gospel, who will not receive a hundredfold now in this time, houses and brothers and sisters and mothers and children and lands, with persecutions, and in the age to come eternal life. But many who are first will be last, and the last first."

Mark 10:17–31

PRAYER OF THANKSGIVING

We thank you God for your deep love and compassion for sinners like us. Through the giving of your Son we are saved from our sin, made new creations in Christ and eternal heirs in your kingdom. How rich a blessing!

Daily Devotion

I will instruct you and teach you in the way you should go; I will counsel you with my eye upon you. Be not like a horse or a mule, without understanding, which must be curbed with bit and bridle, or it will not stay near you. Many are the sorrows of the wicked, but steadfast love surrounds the one who trusts in the LORD. Be glad in the LORD, and rejoice, O righteous, and shout for joy, all you upright in heart!

Psalm 32:8–11

In the first of his ninety-five theses, Martin Luther observed, "When our Lord and Master Jesus Christ said, 'Repent' (Matthew 4:17), he willed the entire life of believers to be one of repentance." Turning from sin and turning to God is an ongoing rhythm in the Christian life. Understanding the various aspects of repentance and putting them together through reflection helps us keep them together in our theology and practice. So let's retrace some of our steps this week.

Repentance is a work of the Holy Spirit. God is the one who calls us to repentance, and it is by his Spirit that we are able to hear and respond in faith. If our repentance were dependent on our initiative, then we would inevitably feel frustrated and weary, or perhaps self-righteous. These are the marks of penance, whereas the mark of the Spirit's work in our lives is joy and peace and hope (Romans 15:13). Moreover, God "condemned sin in the flesh, in order that the righteous requirements of the law might be fulfilled in us, who walk not according to the flesh but according to the Spirit" (Romans 8:3–4). Repentance is a response to God's grace, enabled by his Sprit, and focused on fellowship with him.

Repentance is addressed to God. King David's famous confession is a great example of addressing God: "Have mercy on me, O God, according to your steadfast love; according to your abundant mercy blot out my transgressions. Wash me thoroughly from my iniquity, and cleanse me from my sin! For I know my transgressions, and my sin is ever before me" (Psalm 51:1–3). His transgressions were adultery and murder, two sins clearly against other people. Yet, he says to God: "Against you, you only, have I sinned and done what is evil in your sight" (51:4). This does not nullify his responsibility to others, but simply underscores the primacy of God in all things.

Repentance is walking in the light. There was a time when David walked in darkness, unwilling to see things for what they were. In Psalm

32, he writes: "When I kept silent, my bones wasted away through my groaning all day long. For day and night your hand was heavy upon me; my strength was dried up as by the heat of summer" (32:3–4). Only when he came clean with God did he experience the grace of God: "I acknowledged my sin to you, and I did not cover my iniquity; I said, 'I will confess my transgressions to the LORD,' and you forgave the iniquity of my sin" (v. 5).

Repentance is taking responsibility for our sin. In Psalm 51, David locates the problem: "I know my transgressions, and my sin is ever before me" (v. 3). He does not blame or justify or look for a way out. He goes on: "Behold, I was brought forth in iniquity, and in sin did my mother conceive me" (v. 5). The problem is not just that he sinned, but that he is sinful. It would not be enough to clean the outside of the cup, which is why he seeks a deeper cleansing: "Behold, you delight in truth in the inward being. . . . Purge me with hyssop, and I shall be clean; wash me, and I shall be whiter than snow. . . . Create in me a clean heart, O God, and renew a right spirit within me" (51:6–7, 10).

Repentance is turning to God in faith. In everyday language, repentance means "a change of mind," to reconsider how we are living our lives in light of our new identity and purpose in Christ. We are prone to wander, to pursue life on our terms, to locate our sense of worth and joy and peace outside of God. So the call to repentance is a standing invitation to give up our idolatrous pursuits, and turn to the one true God who restores us to the life for which we were made. We cannot save ourselves.

Repentance is initial and ongoing. You may get in the light and feel very liberated. But then it won't be long until you are unmotivated, feeling the disappointment of another rut. This does not indicate the failure of repentance, but merely teaches us that repentance is both initial and ongoing. Real change always requires a clean break, reaffirmed through subsequent decisions. If you are in a mess, and it has happened over weeks or months or years, it is not going to get cleaned up right away. It's a lifestyle. But there is always hope because of Jesus. When you repent, God himself will "Restore to me the joy of your salvation, and uphold me with a willing spirit" (Psalm 51:12).

REFLECTION QUESTIONS

1. What is God speaking to you about this week? Where is he bringing conviction? What actions do you need to take in response?
2. How has studying repentance this week changed your attitudes and affection for Christ's work on the cross?

CLOSING PRAYER

God of compassion, through your Son, Jesus Christ, you reconciled your people to yourself. Following his example of prayer and fasting, may we obey you with willing hearts and serve one another in holy love through Jesus Christ. Amen.[1]

---

[1] *The Worship Sourcebook*, 549.

SECOND SUNDAY OF LENT

We believe the Word was in the form of God and did not count equality with God a thing to be grasped. He emptied himself, took the form of a servant, and was born in our own likeness. We believe he humbled himself and became obedient unto death. We believe God has highly exalted him, and bestowed on him the name that is above every name. We believe that at the name of Jesus every knee shall bow, in heaven and on earth and under the earth; and every tongue will confess that Jesus Christ is Lord to the glory of God the Father. Amen.[2]

Crown him with many crowns,
the Lamb upon his throne,
Hark! how the·heavenly anthem drowns
all music but its own.
Awake, my soul, and sing
of him who died for thee,
and hail him as thy matchless King
through all eternity.

Crown him the Lord of life,
who triumphed o'er the grave,
and rose victorious in the strife
for those he came to save.
His glories now we sing,
who died, and rose on high,
who died, eternal life to bring,
and lives that death may die.

Crown him the Lord of love;
behold his hands and side,
those wounds, yet visible above,
in beauty glorified.
All hail, Redeemer, hail!
For thou hast died for me;
thy praise and glory shall not fail
throughout eternity.[3]

---

[2] Adapted from Philippians 2:6-11
[3] Matthew Bridges, "Crown Him With Many Crowns", 1851.

WEEK TWO: HUMILITY

Day 11

Daily Readings

CALL TO WORSHIP

Make me to know your ways, O LORD; teach me your paths. Lead me in your truth and teach me, for you are the God of my salvation; for you I wait all the day long. Good and upright is the LORD; therefore he instructs sinners in the way. He leads the humble in what is right, and teaches the humble his way. All the paths of the LORD are steadfast love and faithfulness, for those who keep his covenant and his testimonies.

Psalm 25:4–5, 8–10

CONFESSION

We confess that even though we have been united with Christ, our thoughts and words are divisive. We have been comforted with his love, but have withheld our love from others. We have fellowship with the Spirit of God, yet we still seek our own way. Forsaking unity, we have acted out of selfish ambition. Exalting ourselves, we have sought to be praised. Neglecting our neighbor, we have looked to our own interests above all else. But You, oh Lord, have not withheld your love from us. You became nothing so that we might gain everything. Have mercy upon us, according to your great compassion through Jesus Christ, our Lord. Amen. (Based on Philippians 2.)

GOSPEL OF MARK

And they were on the road, going up to Jerusalem, and Jesus was walking ahead of them. And they were amazed, and those who followed were afraid. And taking the twelve again, he began to tell them what was to happen to him, saying, "See, we are going up to Jerusalem, and the Son of Man will be delivered over to the chief priests and the scribes, and they will condemn him to death and deliver him over to the Gentiles. And they will mock him and spit on him, and flog him and kill him. And after three days he will rise."

Mark 10:32–34

PRAYER OF THANKSGIVING

Jesus humbled himself and became obedient to death on a cross. Through the obedience of Christ we are freed from whatever sin enslaves us. May we boast only in Jesus, our salvation.

Daily Devotion

Though he was in the form of God, [he] did not count equality with God a thing to be grasped, but made himself nothing, taking the form of a servant, being born in the likeness of men. And being found in human form, he humbled himself by becoming obedient to the point of death, even death on a cross.

Philippians 2:6–8

From beginning to end, Jesus's life on earth was marked by humility. Jesus "emptied himself." This is not to say he became something less than God in his humanity, "for in him the whole fullness of deity dwells bodily" (Colossians 2:9). It is to say that he became human, laying down his glorious form to take up a body of flesh. An incomparable condescension.

Why would the Son of God give up his seat at the right hand of the Father for a place at the table with sinners and tax collectors? He did it for us: "The Son of Man came not to be served but to serve, and to give his life as a ransom for many" (Mark 10:45). "Though he was rich, yet for your sake he became poor, so that you by his poverty might become rich" (2 Corinthians 8:9).

Jesus "humbled himself." The emphasis is on obedience to the will of the Father, which was the death of his Son on a cross. An unbearable thought. But it is in his obedience that we see his humility. The night before his crucifixion, Jesus "began to be greatly distressed and troubled. them [the disciples], 'My soul is very sorrowful, even to death.' Remain here and watch. And going a little farther, he fell on the ground and prayed that, if it were possible, the hour might pass from him. And he said, 'Abba, Father, all things are possible for you. Remove this cup from me'" (Mark 14:33–36). The "cup" is Old Testament imagery for the outpouring of God's righteous wrath. Jesus, in the garden, acknowledges what is to come on the cross, where he will take upon himself God's judgment against the sin of the world. Jesus's agony in the garden was more than betrayal or death, both of which are tragic. His deepest agony was that he was about to experience the Father turning away from him—the infinitely perfect and eternally unbroken love between the Father and his beloved Son was about to be broken. The mere taste of it was overwhelming sorrow.

The thought of drinking the cup in full was so dreadful that Jesus asked if there was any way to avoid it. He went to God like a little child who believes that Dad is able to get him out of whatever difficulty he's in. Jesus asked, "Dad, you can do anything ... can you take this cup from me?" For Jesus's whole life, whenever he turned to the Father in prayer, he found comfort and strength. All the light and love of heaven flooded his soul. This time he turns to the Father and "finds hell rather than heaven opened up before him."[4]

It was sorrow unto death. When you see that the mere taste of the cup was enough to throw the Son into this kind of pain, then you are ready in this season to consider what the full experience on the cross must have been like for him. You can begin to understand the depth of humility that says, "Yet not what I will, but what you will" (Mark 14:36).

REFLECTION QUESTIONS

1. What stands out to you the most concerning the humility of Jesus?
2. Do you sense a need to submit to God's will in some area of your life?

---

[4] William Lane, *The Gospel According to Mark: The English Text With Introduction, Exposition, and Notes (New International Commentary on the New Testament)* (Grand Rapids: Eerdmans, 1974).

3. How does the Holy Spirit enable us to move toward humility?

CLOSING PRAYER

Almighty and everlasting God, who, of thy tender love towards mankind, hast sent thy Son our Savior Jesus Christ, to take upon him our flesh, and to suffer death upon the cross, that all mankind should follow the example of his great humility: Mercifully grant, that we may both follow the example of his patience, and also be made partakers of his resurrection; through the same Jesus Christ our Lord.[5]

---

[5] *The Book of Common Prayer*, 168.

Day 12

Daily Readings

CALL TO WORSHIP

Come, everyone who thirsts, come to the waters; and he who has no money, come, buy and eat! Come, buy wine and milk without money and without price. Why do you spend your money for that which is not bread, and your labor for that which does not satisfy? Listen diligently to me, and eat what is good, and delight yourselves in rich food. Incline your ear, and come to me; hear, that your soul may live; and I will make with you an everlasting covenant, my steadfast, sure love for David.

Isaiah 55:1–3

CONFESSION

God of compassion, you are slow to anger and full of mercy, welcoming sinners who return to you with penitent hearts. Receive in your loving embrace all who come home to you. Seat them at your bountiful table of grace, that, with all your children, they may feast with delight on all that satisfies the hungry heart. We ask this in the name of Jesus Christ, our Savior, who lives and reigns with you in the unity of the Holy Spirit, one God, forever and ever. Amen.[6]

GOSPEL OF MARK

And James and John, the sons of Zebedee, came up to him and said to him, "Teacher, we want you to do for us whatever we ask of you." And he said to them, "What do you want me to do for you?" And

---

[6] *The Worship Sourcebook*, 562.

they said to him, "Grant us to sit, one at your right hand and one at your left, in your glory." Jesus said to them, "You do not know what you are asking. Are you able to drink the cup that I drink, or to be baptized with the baptism with which I am baptized?" And they said to him, "We are able." And Jesus said to them, "The cup that I drink you will drink, and with the baptism with which I am baptized, you will be baptized, but to sit at my right hand or at my left is not mine to grant, but it is for those for whom it has been prepared." And when the ten heard it, they began to be indignant at James and John. And Jesus called them to him and said to them, "You know that those who are considered rulers of the Gentiles lord it over them, and their great ones exercise authority over them. But it shall not be so among you. But <u>whoever would be great among you must be your servant</u>, and whoever would be first among you <u>must be slave of all.</u> For even the Son of Man came not to be served but to serve, and to give his life as a ransom for many."

Mark 10:35–45

PRAYER OF THANKSGIVING

In our thirst for fulfillment, Jesus Christ is our righteousness and life. We delight ourselves in Jesus Christ alone., who has ransomed us from our futile ways with his precious blood and comforted us with his wounds. Praise Jesus!

Daily Devotion

Do nothing from rivalry or conceit, but in humility count others more significant than yourselves. Let each of you look not only to his own interests, but also to the interests of others.

Philippians 2:3–4

Paul tells the Philippians to live this way because this is the way Jesus lived. Jesus is God, but he became a servant. He is the righteous judge, but gave himself up to the verdict of wicked men. This is the humility of our Lord: He had nothing to gain; yet he gave up all he had.

Everyone esteems the virtue of humility, but to step into the reality of our lives is to remember how contrary it is to our thinking. In so many ways, we are accustomed to building ourselves up—proving our worth, impressing people, vying to be noticed and honored. Ironically, we even hope to be recognized for our humility. Try to give up wanting attention or praise for a day, and you will realize how pervasive our desire is to be lifted up.

The desire to be lifted up is rooted in a lack of faith. We are worried about what others think because we are not convinced that God delights in us (Psalm 149:4). We are anxious because we do not believe God will meet our needs (Matthew 6:32). We vie for attention because we do not think God rewards what is done in secret (Matthew 6:6). We compare ourselves to others because we forget that Jesus is our righteousness (1 Corinthians 1:30).

The simple practice of self-denial in Lent teaches us that those who trust God to meet their needs are free to consider the needs of others. They discover this gospel paradox: As long as I'm looking to get my needs met, I will never get my needs met. But when, by the power of the Holy Spirit, I begin to meet the needs of others, I find that God graciously takes care of my needs in the process (2 Corinthians 9:6–8). The grace of God turns us into servants. Instead of demanding that we be served, we joyfully lay down our rights to serve God and others (Mark 10:43–45).

Repentance must begin with humility, because even our repentance can be motivated by pride. We may turn from our ways only to protect our image or self-righteousness. So we look to Christ, who did not give himself to the approval of men, but entrusted himself to the Father (1 Peter 2:23).

REFLECTION QUESTIONS

1. From whom do you want approval or attention?
2. How does a relationship with God satisfy those desires?
3. How does the Holy Spirit help us exalt Jesus? (John 16:12–15)

CLOSING PRAYER

O God of grace, you have imputed my sin to my substitute and you have imputed his righteousness to my soul, clothing me with a bridegroom's robe, decking me with jewels of holiness. But in my Christian walk I am still in rags; my best prayers are stained with sin; my penitential tears are so much impurity; my confessions of wrong are so many aggravations of sin; my receiving the Spirit is tinctured with selfishness. I need to repent of my repentance.[7]

---

[7] Arthur Bennett, *The Valley of Vision: A Collection of Puritan Prayers and Devotions* (Edinburgh: Banner of Truth Trust, 2007), 136.

Day 13

Daily Readings

CALL TO WORSHIP

"Trust in the LORD forever, for the LORD GOD is an everlasting rock. For he has humbled the inhabitants of the height, the lofty city. He lays it low, lays it low to the ground, casts it to the dust. The foot tramples it, the feet of the poor, the steps of the needy." The path of the righteous is level; you make level the way of the righteous. In the path of your judgments, O LORD, we wait for you; your name and remembrance are the desire of our soul. My soul yearns for you in the night; my spirit within me earnestly seeks you. For when your judgments are in the earth, the inhabitants of the world learn righteousness. O LORD, you will ordain peace for us, for you have indeed done for us all our works.

Isaiah 26:4–9, 12

CONFESSION

God of mercy, you sent Jesus Christ to seek and save the lost. We confess that we have strayed from you and turned aside from your way. We are misled by pride, for we see ourselves pure when we are stained and great when we are small. We have failed in love, neglected justice, and ignored your truth. Have mercy, O God, and forgive our sin. Return us to paths of righteousness through Jesus Christ, our Savior. Amen.[8]

GOSPEL OF MARK

And they came to Jericho. And as he was leaving Jericho with his disciples and a great crowd, Bartimaeus, a blind beggar, the son of

---

[8] *The Worship Sourcebook*, 563.

Timaeus, was sitting by the roadside. And when he heard that it was Jesus of Nazareth, he began to cry out and say, "Jesus, Son of David, have mercy on me!" And many rebuked him, telling him to be silent. But he cried out all the more, "Son of David, have mercy on me!" And Jesus stopped and said, "Call him." And they called the blind man, saying to him, "Take heart. Get up; he is calling you." And throwing off his cloak, he sprang up and came to Jesus. And Jesus said to him, "What do you want me to do for you?" And the blind man said to him, "Rabbi, let me recover my sight." And Jesus said to him, "Go your way; your faith has made you well." And immediately he recovered his sight and followed him on the way.

Mark 10:46–52

PRAYER OF THANKSGIVING

Lord Jesus, you bore the wrath of God, so that we who hope in God are assured of his mercy. God's judgment fell on you in order that we, the guilty, might go free. By God's grace we are converted, and given the ability to repent of sin, to walk in new life, and to will what is good. Praise to Jesus, our substitutionary Lamb.

Daily Devotion

For Christ also suffered once for sins, the righteous for the unrighteous, that he might bring us to God.

1 Peter 3:18

Pride is the great enemy of humility. Bob Thune observes:

"The brashest expressions of pride are easy to spot: the athlete who boasts about her talent, the arrogant entrepreneur who flaunts his achievements, or the well-connected neighbor who name-drops in every conversation. Most of us are smart enough to avoid appearing prideful in these obvious ways. But that's just the problem. We can avoid looking prideful without actually killing our pride."[9]

---

[9] Robert H. Thune and Will Walker, *The Gospel Centered Community*, (Greensboro, NC: New Growth Press, 2013).

To put pride to death, we must "trace this serpent in all its turnings and windings."[10] That is, we must get a fuller picture of what pride is and how it looks.

On the one hand, the Bible tells us that pride often manifests itself as arrogance: the apostle John refers to this as "the pride of life" (1 John 2:16). On the other hand, the Bible affirms that pride can manifest itself as subtle self-centeredness, looking out for your own personal interests (Philippians 2:4).

Either way, the essence of pride is self-concern. It may manifest itself as arrogance and boasting, or as self-protection and fear of people—but it's pride either way. If we want to cultivate humility, we must put pride to death. How? By looking to Jesus as both our model and our mediator.

"Looking to Jesus" is our way of saying consider who he is and what he has done, let it sink in and stir your affections. But this is not something we can do on our own. We need the Holy Spirit to lift our eyes and make real to us the person and work of Jesus. So let us look to Jesus with faith, trusting the Spirit's power to teach and change us.

Jesus is our model, because though he had every reason to be prideful (he was perfect), he chose instead the path of humility. Scripture commands us to follow his example: "Have this mind among yourselves, which is yours in Christ Jesus, who, though he was in the form of God, did not count equality with God a thing to be grasped, but made himself nothing, taking the form of a servant, being born in the likeness of men" (Philippians 2:5–7).

One cannot be like Jesus without humility, but if we merely try harder to be like him, we will miss the gospel. The heart of the good news is that we can be more like Jesus only if, and because, we are united with him. "You, however, are not in the flesh but in the Spirit, if in fact the Spirit of God dwells in you. Anyone who does not have the Spirit of Christ does not belong to him. But if Christ is in you, although the body is dead because of sin, the Spirit is life because of righteousness. If the Spirit of him who raised Jesus from the dead dwells in you, he

---

[10] John Owen, *Temptation and Sin* (Mulberry, IN: Sovereign Grace Publishers, 2001).

who raised <u>Christ Jesus</u> from the dead <u>will also give life</u> to your mortal bodies through his Spirit who dwells in you" (Romans 8:9–11).

<u>Jesus is our mediator, because he stood in our place</u>. Jesus "humbled himself to the point of death, even death on a cross" (Philippians 2:8)—<u>taking our shame and guilt upon himself, and enduring the wrath of God against sin</u>, so that those who humbly come to him can be forgiven and reconciled to God. This is the Good News of Easter!

Look to Christ, who was humble in life and broken in death to set you free from self-concern.

REFLECTION QUESTIONS

1. What are the major areas of self-concern in your heart?
2. How does the example of Jesus inspire and challenge you?
3. How does the Holy Spirit enable us to follow his example?

CLOSING PRAYER

Humble my heart before thee, and replenish it with thy choicest gifts. As water rests not on barren hill summits, but flows down to fertilize lowest vales, so make me the lowest of the lowly, that my spiritual riches may exceedingly abound. When I leave duties undone, may condemning thought strip me of pride, deepen in me devotion to thy service, and quicken me to more watchful care. <u>When I am tempted to think highly</u> of myself, <u>grant me to see the wily power of my spiritual enemy</u>; Help me to stand with wary eye on the watchtower of faith, and to cling with determined grasp to my humble Lord; If I fall let me hide myself in my Redeemer's righteousness, and when I escape, may I ascribe all deliverance to thy grace. Keep me humble, meek, lowly.[11]

---

[11] *The Valley of Vision*, 161.

Day 14

Daily Readings

CALL TO WORSHIP

Rejoice greatly, O daughter of Zion! Shout aloud, O daughter of Jerusalem! Behold, your king is coming to you; righteous and having salvation is he, humble and mounted on a donkey, on a colt, the foal of a donkey. I will cut off the chariot from Ephraim and the war horse from Jerusalem; and the battle bow shall be cut off, and he shall speak peace to the nations; his rule shall be from sea to sea, and from the River to the ends of the earth.

Zechariah 9:9–10

CONFESSION

Loving God, you rode a donkey and came in peace, humbled yourself and gave yourself for us. We confess our lack of humility. As you entered Jerusalem, the crowds shouted "Hosanna: 'Save us now!'" On Good Friday they shouted "Crucify!" We confess our praise is often empty. We sing "Hosanna," but cry "Crucify." As the crowd laid their palms in front of you, you took no glory for yourself. We confess that we want to be accepted and take the easy way. We do not stay true to your will. Forgive us, Lord, and help us to follow in the way of obedience. Amen.[12]

GOSPEL OF MARK

Now when they drew near to Jerusalem, to Bethphage and Bethany, at the Mount of Olives, Jesus sent two of his disciples and said to them, "Go into the village in front of you, and immediately as you

---

[12] *The Worship Sourcebook*, 586.

enter it you will find a colt tied, on which no one has ever sat. Untie it and bring it. If anyone says to you, 'Why are you doing this?' say, 'The Lord has need of it and will send it back here immediately.'" And they went away and found a colt tied at a door outside in the street, and they untied it. And some of those standing there said to them, "What are you doing, untying the colt?" And they told them what Jesus had said, and they let them go. And they brought the colt to Jesus and threw their cloaks on it, and he sat on it. And many spread their cloaks on the road, and others spread leafy branches that they had cut from the fields. And those who went before and those who followed were shouting, "Hosanna! Blessed is he who comes in the name of the Lord! Blessed is the coming kingdom of our father David! Hosanna in the highest!"

Mark 11:1–10

PRAYER OF THANKSGIVING

Lord, you set your face toward Jerusalem, and you entered as a lowly king. You came to save us. You came to bring us peace, hope, and life. Hosanna in the highest!

Daily Devotion

Know that the LORD, he is God! It is he who made us, and we are his; we are his people, and the sheep of his pasture.

Psalm 100:3

Pride is thinking of ourselves more highly than we ought to think (Romans 12:3). However, humility is not thinking less of ourselves than we ought to think, but simply thinking of ourselves less. We are to think of ourselves with "sober judgment, each according to the measure of faith that God has assigned" (Romans 12:3). In other words, the humble person knows who he is, and whose he is.

This is the secret to Jesus's remarkable humility. Even as a child, Jesus was about his Father's business. People always questioned his identity, but he was not thrown off by their doubt or criticism (Mark 8:27–30). When the crowds were flocking to Jesus, he withdrew to pray. He did not need the approval of people because he was rooted in the words that came down from heaven: "You are my beloved Son; with you I am well pleased" (Mark 1:11). Without any hubris, Jesus could say, "I am the way, and the truth, and the life" (John 14:6). Without self-concern, Jesus could say, "The Son of Man will be delivered over to the chief priests and the scribes, and they will condemn him to death" (Mark 10:33).

This is not to say that any of this was easy. Jesus was "a man of sorrows, and acquainted with grief" (Isaiah 53:3). The point is that he was able to endure such difficulty because of his sense of identity and purpose. In the same way, people like Abraham and Moses "died in faith, not having received the things promised, but having seen them and greeted them from afar, and having acknowledged that they were strangers and exiles on the earth" (Hebrews 11:13).

In contrast to pride and fear, the humility we see in Jesus is marked by dependence and confidence. If we aspire to walk in this path, we will have to think with sober judgment. We will have to be clear-eyed about who we are and whose we are. Where do we get this kind of clarity?

The gospel tells us who we are: We are made in the image of God, created in his likeness for his glory. This truth speaks to both our dignity and our dependence. Before and after the fall, people need God in every aspect of life, "for 'in him we live and move and have our being'" (Acts 17:28).

The gospel tells us whose we are: We belong to God, body and soul. He is our Maker, to whom we belong by virtue of design. He is our Father, to whom we belong to by means of adoption. He is our Master, and we are his servants. He is our king, and we are his subjects. Nothing "will be able to separate us from the love of God in Christ Jesus our Lord" (Romans 8:39).

It is so easy to forget who we are and whose we are, which is why we need a community that speaks the truth in love to one another (Ephesians 4:15). To be humble means we are willing to be seen as we are, by God and people. In order to help us see, God has often given us the very people from whom we are trying to hide our true selves.

If we aspire to love one another, then we also need to be humble enough to accept and speak to whatever the light reveals. Through the work of the Spirit, we are becoming less concerned with our prestige, and less demanding of our "rights." Pride is being starved because we are letting go of our need to be right and our desires to be recognized. On the journey to the cross, we are being liberated from the solitary confinement of self-concern.

REFLECTION QUESTIONS

1. How does your community help you know who and whose you are?
2. How does the Holy Spirit assure us of our identity in Christ? (Romans 8:14–17)

CLOSING PRAYER

O Lord Jesus Christ, you are enthroned in the majesty of heaven, yet you gave up that heavenly perfection to become a servant. We adore you for laying aside your glory and clothing yourself in complete humility as one of us. We praise you for the example of washing your disciples' feet. Teach us to do as you have done. Deliver us from pride, jealousy, and ambition, and make us ready to serve one another in lowliness for your sake, O Jesus Christ, our Lord and Savior. Amen.[13]

---

[13] *The Worship Sourcebook*, 595.

Day 15

Daily Readings

CALL TO WORSHIP

My soul magnifies the Lord, and my spirit rejoices in God my Savior, for he has looked on the humble estate of his servant. For behold, from now on all generations will call me blessed; for he who is mighty has done great things for me, and holy is his name. And his mercy is for those who fear him from generation to generation. He has shown strength with his arm; he has scattered the proud in the thoughts of their hearts; he has brought down the mighty from their thrones and exalted those of humble estate; he has filled the hungry with good things, and the rich he has sent away empty. He has helped his servant Israel, in remembrance of his mercy, as he spoke to our fathers, to Abraham and to his offspring forever.

Luke 1:46–55

CONFESSION

Word of God Incarnate, you came to this world to accomplish salvation. By your grace you call us to repent, to be crucified with you, that we might be raised as new creations. But we confess that we often do not live as renewed people. We confess that often we "go with the flow" instead of stemming sin's tide. Forgive us when we do not show evidence of renewal. Forgive us when we let the fruit of the Spirit be choked by the weeds of evil. You have made us your children, members of your kingdom. Help us to show evidence of that every day as we work to bring your justice, peace, gentleness, goodness, love, joy, and hope to all we meet. For Jesus's sake, Amen.[14]

GOSPEL OF MARK

And he entered Jerusalem and went into the temple. And when he had looked around at everything, as it was already late, he went out to Bethany with the twelve. On the following day, when they came from Bethany, he was hungry. And seeing in the distance a fig tree in leaf, he went to see if he could find anything on it. When he came to it, he found nothing but leaves, for it was not the season for figs. And he said to it, "May no one ever eat fruit from you again." And his disciples heard it. And they came to Jerusalem. And he entered the temple and began to drive out those who sold and those who bought in the temple, and he overturned the tables of the money-changers and the seats of those who sold pigeons. And he would not allow anyone to carry anything through the temple. And he was teaching them and saying to them, "Is it not written, 'My house shall be called a house of prayer for all the nations'? But you have made it a den of robbers." And the chief priests and the scribes heard it and were seeking a way to destroy him, for they feared him, because all the crowd was astonished at his teaching. And when evening came they went out of the city.

Mark 11:11–19

PRAYER OF THANKSGIVING

Lord Jesus, you are the new and better temple—God dwelling among us. In you the curtain has been torn in two and a new and living way has been opened up to us. You are Emmanuel, God with us.

Daily Devotion

James and John, the sons of Zebedee, came up to him and said to him, "Teacher, we want you to do for us whatever we ask of you."

Mark 10:35

---

[14] *The Worship Sourcebook*, 566.

How's that for humble prayer? "Before I say what I want, I want you to say you'll do it." We are good at telling God what we want, but we are not very good at learning what God wants. That kind of learning takes patience, reflection, study, obedience, and most of all it requires deep humility. It's much easier just to go with what we think is best.

Jesus entertains the request: "'What do you want me to do for you?' And they said to him, 'Grant us to sit, one at your right hand and one at your left, in your glory'" (10:36–37).

It was an absurd request, but not to them of course. They had it in their heads that Jesus would deliver them from their oppressors and establish an earthly reign. Further, they saw themselves as high-ranking officials in the new regime.

Their perception of reality and their notion of what was good and right prevented them from understanding what Jesus had just told them: "The Son of Man will be delivered over to the chief priests and the scribes, and they will condemn him to death and deliver him over to the Gentiles. And they will mock him and spit on him, and flog him and kill him" (10:33–34).

If you come to God on your terms, expecting him to fit into your worldview and align with the way you think things ought to be, you are starting off on the wrong foot, and that will lead you down the wrong path. Like Jesus's first disciples you will end up thinking and saying things that are exactly the opposite of what real life in God's new kingdom is all about.

Jesus said to them, "You do not know what you are asking. Are you able to drink the cup that I drink, or to be baptized with the baptism with which I am baptized?" (10:38). In other words: "My glory is not what you think it is. And the path of glory is certainly not what you think it is." Just like we often do, these brothers had mistaken importance for significance.

Importance speaks to the value we derive from things like position, status, and the esteem of others. It is about building our brand: dropping names, getting close to popular people, flaunting knowledge, looking busy, defining spiritual maturity by activity and achievement, exalting public gifts above the others. Significance speaks to the value we add to people and culture. It's about building others up: remembering their name, drawing near to the fringe, teaching others, being accessible, defining spiritual maturity by love for others, exalting Jesus as the head of the body, and appreciating the contribution of each member.

The "cup" refers to the suffering that Jesus was about to endure. Before he could be exalted to his throne, he had to be hung on a tree. The disciples could not die the mediator's death, but they would drink from the cup of his suffering. Greatness in the kingdom always involves a cross.

It was a teaching moment for the disciples, and for us: "Whoever would be great among you must be your servant, and whoever would be first among you must be slave of all. For even the Son of Man came not to be served but to serve, and to give his life as a ransom for many" (Mark 10:45).

Humility is not the absence of position and power. It is the use of such things for the good of others. If we can get our minds and affections around the true greatness of Jesus and his cross—and what that means for us—then we can be great in the kingdom of God.

REFLECTION QUESTIONS

1. What gets noticed and praised in your family, workplace, and church?
2. What does true greatness look like in those environments?
3. You may feel like God isn't speaking to you about various things, but have you let go of what you want so that you might be able to listen with unbiased ears?

CLOSING PRAYER

Father of Jesus, Dawn returns, but without thy light within, no outward light can profit. Give me the saving lamp of thy Spirit that I may see thee, the God of my salvation, the delight of my soul, rejoicing over me in love. I commend my heart to thy watchful care, for I know its treachery and power. Guard its every portal from the wily enemy, give me quick discernment of his deadly arts, help me to recognize his bold disguise as an angel of light, and bid him begone. . . . Help me to walk as Jesus walked, my only Saviour and perfect model, his mind my inward guest, his meekness my covering garb. Let my happy place be amongst the poor in spirit, my delight the gentle ranks of the meek. Let me always esteem others better than myself, and find in true humility an heirdom to two worlds.[1]

---

[1] *The Valley of Vision*, 249.

Day 16

Daily Readings

CALL TO WORSHIP

Not to us, O LORD, not to us, but to your name give glory, for the sake of your steadfast love and your faithfulness! Why should the nations say, "Where is their God?" Our God is in the heavens; he does all that he pleases. Their idols are silver and gold, the work of human hands. They have mouths, but do not speak; eyes, but do not see. They have ears, but do not hear; noses, but do not smell. They have hands, but do not feel; feet, but do not walk; and they do not make a sound in their throat. Those who make them become like them; so do all who trust in them. The heavens are the LORD's heavens, but the earth he has given to the children of man. The dead do not praise the LORD, nor do any who go down into silence. But we will bless the LORD from this time forth and forevermore. Praise the LORD!

Psalm 115:1–8, 16–18

CONFESSION

Almighty God, in Jesus Christ you love us, but we have not loved you. You have opened your heart to us, and in our pride we have spurned your care. You have given us all things, and we have squandered your gifts. We have grieved you and caused hurt to others, and we are not worthy to be called your children. Have mercy on us, O Lord, for we are ashamed and sorry for all we have done to displease you. Cleanse us from our sin and receive us again into your household, that we might nevermore stray from your love but always remain within the sound of your voice. Amen.[2]

---

[2] *The Worship Sourcebook*, 567.

GOSPEL OF MARK

As they passed by in the morning, they saw the fig tree withered away to its roots. And Peter remembered and said to him, "Rabbi, look! The fig tree that you cursed has withered." And Jesus answered them, "Have faith in God. Truly, I say to you, whoever says to this mountain, 'Be taken up and thrown into the sea,' and does not doubt in his heart, but believes that what he says will come to pass, it will be done for him. Therefore I tell you, whatever you ask in prayer, believe that you have received it, and it will be yours. And whenever you stand praying, forgive, if you have anything against anyone, so that your Father also who is in heaven may forgive you your trespasses."

Mark 11:20–26

PRAYER OF THANKSGIVING

Thank you Father for the blessing of faith. You have forgiven our trespasses, delivering us from our biggest enemies of Satan, sin, and death. We are assured that we can come confidently to you in all things because you have the power to save and you have the desire to restore. To your name, O Lord, be the glory.

Daily Devotion

Now before the Feast of the Passover, when Jesus knew that his hour had come to depart out of this world to the Father, having loved his own who were in the world, he loved them to the end. During supper, when the devil had already put it into the heart of Judas Iscariot, Simon's son, to betray him, Jesus, knowing that the Father had given all things into his hands, and that he had come from God and was going back to God, rose from supper. He laid aside his outer garments, and taking a towel, tied it around his waist. Then he poured water into a basin and began to wash the disciples' feet and to wipe them with the towel that was wrapped around him.

John 13:1–5

Jesus stood among them as the one who served. Humility on display.

Washing feet was a necessary, but dirty job. It was reserved for the lowest ranking servants. That's what makes this so shocking. Jesus had the knowledge of a prophet and the power of a king, yet he acted like a servant.

This scene comes on the heels of the disciples' argument about who was the greatest. So there they were in the middle of supper, reclining around the table with their dirty feet, and Jesus—the only truly great one among them—got up to serve them. He took off his outer garments and wrapped a towel around his waist (adopting the dress of a slave), and he began to wash his disciples' feet.

Peter, as you would imagine, had something to say about it: "Lord, do you wash my feet?" (13:6). Peter sees how backwards this is, and insists that Jesus not wash his feet. It is awkward for a king to attend to the needs of the servants. Like Peter, we do not want to be the kind of people who need serving. We can take care of ourselves. Do you see how prideful that is?

But Jesus says, "If I do not wash you, you have no share with me." Now we begin to see the layers of Jesus's ministry here. He is really washing their dirty feet, but he is also teaching them about the spiritual cleansing that we need and that Jesus will accomplish on the cross. The picture is that we are dirty in sin, stained through and through. Jesus sees our helplessness and says, You cannot clean yourself up. Unless you let me wash you, you can never be clean. Unless I die for you, you can't live with me.

Jesus stands before you as the one who makes you clean. Put down your proud humility and be washed.

Peter swings the pendulum to the other side: "Lord, not my feet only but also my hands and my head!" (13:9). First, he had a hard time receiving what Jesus was wanted to do. Then, he had a hard time resting in what Jesus had done. Jesus assured him: "you are clean" (13:10).

Has Jesus died for you sin? Have you received his free offer of salvation? Then you are clean.

Later in the conversation, Peter swears his undying allegiance to Jesus (13:37), to which Jesus replies, Actually, you are going to deny me three times before morning comes (13:38). Jesus knew this was going to happen, yet he said to Peter, "You are clean."

Our standing before God is not about what we have done or not done, what we will do or not do, but rather on what Jesus had done for us in his life, death, and resurrection. He took on "the form of a servant" and "he humbled himself by becoming obedient to the point of death" (Philippians 2:7–8).

Jesus came to serve—to heal, to feed, to make more wine, to wash feet, and to die. As we humbly receive the fullness and sufficiency of his love, the Holy Spirit fills us with this same selfless love in service to others.

REFLECTION QUESTIONS

1. In what ways do you struggle to receive God's gracious help?
2. In what ways do you struggle to rest in his acceptance of you?
3. Who can you move toward in the power of the Spirit, to serve them as you have been served?

CLOSING PRAYER

O thou God of all grace, make me more thankful, more humble. Inspire me with a deep sense of my unworthiness arising from the depravity of my nature, my omitted duties, my unimproved advantages, thy commands violated by me. With all my calls to gratitude and joy may I remember that I have reason for sorrow and humiliation; O give me repentance unto life. Cement my oneness with my blessed Lord, that faith may adhere to him more immovably, that love may entwine itself round him more tightly, that his Spirit may pervade every fibre of my being. Then send me out to make him known to my fellow men.[3]

---

[3] *The Valley of Vision*, 327.

THIRD SUNDAY OF LENT

By his resurrection he has overcome death so that he might make us share in the righteousness he won for us by his death. By his power we too are already now resurrected to a new life. Christ's resurrection is a guarantee of our glorious resurrection.[4]

Jesus Christ is the hope of God's world. In his death, the justice of God is established; forgiveness of sin is proclaimed. On the day of his resurrection, the tomb was empty; his disciples saw him; death was defeated; new life had come. God's purpose for the world was sealed.[5]

Man of Sorrows! what a name
For the Son of God, Who came
Ruined sinners to reclaim.
Hallelujah! What a Savior!

Bearing shame and scoffing rude,
In my place condemned He stood;
Sealed my pardon with His blood.
Hallelujah! What a Savior!

Guilty, vile, and helpless we;
Spotless Lamb of God was He;
Full atonement can it be?
Hallelujah! What a Savior!

Lifted up was He to die;
"It is finished!" was His cry;
Now in heaven exalted high.
Hallelujah! What a Savior!

When He comes, our glorious King,
All His ransomed home to bring,
Then anew His song we'll sing:
Hallelujah! What a Savior![6]

---

[4] Heidelberg Catechism, Question 45
[5] *Our Song of Hope*, St. 4, (Grand Rapids: Eerdmans, 1975).
[6] Philip Bliss, "Man of Sorrows, What a Name", 1875.

WEEK THREE:
SUFFERING

Day 17

Daily Readings

CALL TO WORSHIP

Blessed be the God and Father of our Lord Jesus Christ! According to his great mercy, he has caused us to be born again to a living hope through the resurrection of Jesus Christ from the dead, to an inheritance that is imperishable, undefiled, and unfading, kept in heaven for you, who by God's power are being guarded through faith for a salvation ready to be revealed in the last time. In this you rejoice, though now for a little while, if necessary, you have been grieved by various trials, so that the tested genuineness of your faith—more precious than gold that perishes though it is tested by fire—may be found to result in praise and glory and honor at the revelation of Jesus Christ. Though you have not seen him, you love him. Though you do not now see him, you believe in him and rejoice with joy that is inexpressible and filled with glory, obtaining the outcome of your faith, the salvation of your souls.

1 Peter 1:3–9

CONFESSION

Holy Lord, I have sinned times without number, and been guilty of pride and unbelief, of failure to find thy mind in thy Word, of neglect to seek thee in my daily life. My transgressions and shortcomings present me with a list of accusations, But I bless thee that they will not stand against me, for all have been laid on Christ. Go on to subdue my corruptions, and grant me grace to live above them. Let not the passions of the flesh nor lustings of the mind bring my spirit into subjection, but do thou rule over me in liberty and power.[7]

GOSPEL OF MARK

And they came again to Jerusalem. And as he was walking in the temple, the chief priests and the scribes and the elders came to him, and they said to him, "By what authority are you doing these things, or who gave you this authority to do them?" Jesus said to them, "I will ask you one question; answer me, and I will tell you by what authority I do these things. Was the baptism of John from heaven or from man? Answer me." And they discussed it with one another, saying, "If we say, 'From heaven,' he will say, 'Why then did you not believe him?' But shall we say, 'From man'?"—they were afraid of the people, for they all held that John really was a prophet. So they answered Jesus, "We do not know." And Jesus said to them, "Neither will I tell you by what authority I do these things."

Mark 11:27–33

PRAYER OF THANKSGIVING

Almighty God, we praise you as a God of authority and power. You have the power to condemn, and yet you have redeemed us in Christ. You have the power to curse, and yet you have blessed us in Christ. You have the power to cast off, and yet you have drawn near to us in Christ. Our hearts are filled with joy.

Daily Devotion

As he passed by, he saw a man blind from birth. And his disciples asked him, "Rabbi, who sinned, this man or his parents, that he was born blind?" Jesus answered, "It was not that this man sinned, or his parents, but that the works of God might be displayed in him."

John 9:1–3

Lent is the season leading up to Easter. It is a time of preparation and repentance in which we remember Jesus's suffering and anticipate his resurrection.

---

[7] *The Valley of Vision*, 138.

You may have heard people talk about giving something up for Lent. Throughout history, Christians have observed Lent by fasting, or other acts of self-denial. The danger with tradition, of course, is that it can become mere ritual, or even a source of pride. We want to recapture a spirit of faith in this season.

The point of fasting or self-denial is not to manufacture some kind of suffering. These things simply remind us of the suffering Jesus endured, and draw our attention to the sufficiency of God's grace in our lives.

Unlike repentance and humility, which happen in and through us, suffering and persecution simply happen to us. The subject raises a difficult question: Why does God allow us to suffer? We are always searching for answers to this question, for ourselves and for our world. Not knowing "why" is part of the suffering.

One day when Jesus and his disciples were walking, they passed by a man blind from birth. "And his disciples asked him, 'Rabbi, who sinned, this man or his parents, that he was born blind?'" (John 9:2). They were looking for answers.

It was commonly thought that God blesses those who live piously, and conversely, that suffering was the result of sins that had been committed.

We see this mindset revealed by Job's friends in the book of Job. In truth, Job was being tested with adversity because of his piety, and not because of sin (Job 1:1–12). Job's friends persisted in trying to force him to confess that his suffering was the result of some sin he had committed. If he just forsook his sin, they insisted, then God would again bless him.

Perhaps Asaph had the same assumptions about prosperity and poverty. He was frustrated and angry with God because the wicked appeared to prosper while the pious did not (Psalm 73:1–14).

This is why the disciples framed the question the way they did. Their explanation for suffering was that someone was being punished for sin. But Jesus answered, "It was not that this man sinned, or his parents, but that the works of God might be displayed in him" (John 9:3).

Jesus was not offering a trite explanation of all suffering, but rather pointing to his own suffering that would explain the love of God. Jesus endured suffering, not because he sinned, but because "all have sinned and fall short of the glory of God" (Romans 3:23). He did this so that the works of God might be displayed in him, "whom God put forward as a propitiation by his blood, to be received by faith. This was to show God's righteousness, because in his divine forbearance he had passed over former sins. It was to show his righteousness at the present time, so that he might be just and the justifier of the one who has faith in Jesus" (3:25–26).

We do not have all the answers about why we suffer, but we do know what the answer cannot be. It cannot be that God doesn't see or care, for he sent his own Son to enter into our suffering. And it cannot be a hopeless situation, for he conquered sin and death by raising his Son from the dead.

REFLECTION QUESTIONS

1. How does the reality of suffering challenge your faith?
2. How have you tried to explain suffering?
3. How does Jesus's death and resurrection give you strength and hope?

CLOSING PRAYER

Help me to be resolute and Christ-contained. Never let me wander from the path of obedience to thy will. Strengthen me for the battles ahead. Give me courage for all the trials, and grace for all the joys. Help me to be a holy, happy person, free from every wrong desire, from everything contrary to thy mind. Grant me more and more of the resurrection life: may it rule me, may I walk in its power, and be strengthened through its influence.[8]

---

[8] *The Valley of Vision*, 173.

Day 18

Daily Readings

CALL TO WORSHIP

In the year that King Uzziah died I saw the Lord sitting upon a throne, high and lifted up; and the train of his robe filled the temple. Above him stood the seraphim. Each had six wings: with two he covered his face, and with two he covered his feet, and with two he flew. And one called to another and said: "Holy, holy, holy is the LORD of hosts; the whole earth is full of his glory!" And the foundations of the thresholds shook at the voice of him who called, and the house was filled with smoke. And I said: "Woe is me! For I am lost; for I am a man of unclean lips, and I dwell in the midst of a people of unclean lips; for my eyes have seen the King, the LORD of hosts!" Then one of the seraphim flew to me, having in his hand a burning coal that he had taken with tongs from the altar. And he touched my mouth and said: "Behold, this has touched your lips; your guilt is taken away, and your sin atoned for."

Isaiah 6:1–7

CONFESSION

If you kept a record of sins, O Lord, who could stand? But with you there is forgiveness; therefore you are feared. I wait for the Lord, my soul waits, and in his Word I put my hope. My soul waits for the Lord more than watchmen wait for the morning, more than watchmen wait for the morning. Almighty God, our Redeemer, in our weakness we have failed to be your messengers of forgiveness and hope. Renew us by your Holy Spirit, that we may follow your commands and proclaim your reign of love, through Jesus Christ, our Lord, who lives and reigns with you and the Holy Spirit, one God, now and forever. Amen.[9]

GOSPEL OF MARK

And he began to speak to them in parables. "A man planted a vineyard and put a fence around it and dug a pit for the winepress and built a tower, and leased it to tenants and went into another country. When the season came, he sent a servant to the tenants to get from them some of the fruit of the vineyard. And they took him and beat him and sent him away empty-handed. Again he sent to them another servant, and they struck him on the head and treated him shamefully. And he sent another, and him they killed. And so with many others: some they beat, and some they killed. He had still one other, a beloved son. Finally he sent him to them, saying, 'They will respect my son.' But those tenants said to one another, 'This is the heir. Come, let us kill him, and the inheritance will be ours.' And they took him and killed him and threw him out of the vineyard. What will the owner of the vineyard do? He will come and destroy the tenants and give the vineyard to others. Have you not read this Scripture: "'The stone that the builders rejected has become the cornerstone; this was the Lord's doing, and it is marvelous in our eyes'?" And they were seeking to arrest him but feared the people, for they perceived that he had told the parable against them. So they left him and went away.

Mark 12:1–12

PRAYER OF THANKSGIVING

Holy and merciful God, thank you for removing our guilt, atoning for our sin, and renewing us by your Spirit. You are the Holy One!

Daily Devotion

Therefore, since we have been justified by faith, we have peace with God through our Lord Jesus Christ. Through him we have also obtained access by faith into this grace in which we stand, and we rejoice in hope of the glory of God. More than that, we rejoice in our sufferings, knowing that suffering produces endurance, and endurance produces character, and character produces hope, and

[9] *The Worship Sourcebook*, 560.

hope does not put us to shame, <u>because God's love has been poured</u> <u>into our hearts through the Holy Spirit who has been given to us.</u>
Romans 5:1–5

Whenever I try to make sense of suffering, I end up in the same dilemma. On one hand, I know that my hardships and afflictions are relatively insignificant compared to what I see around me; much less, what I am aware of around the world. On the other hand, I cannot deny that I get sick, stretched, slandered, and snubbed. Privileged as they are, I feel burdened by my circumstances and frustrated with my struggle against sin. It's dishonest to say I don't suffer, at least from my perspective.

So how are we to view the various forms of hardship and trials that we face? What is the relationship between our faith and suffering?

Some teach that Jesus suffered so we wouldn't have to, <u>but our experience</u> <u>and the New Testament tells us that suffering is inevitable. Jesus himself</u> <u>said we would have trouble in this world</u> (John 16:33). It is more than physical hardship. It's also emotional pain, relational woes, soul unrest, and spiritual attack. <u>Jesus's death does not take away our suffering,</u> but <u>it gives profound meaning and purpose to it.</u>

Consider James's exhortation to those who suffer: "Count it all joy, my brothers, when you meet trials of various kinds, for you know that the <u>testing of your faith produces steadfastnes</u>s. And let steadfastness have its full effect, that you may be perfect and complete, lacking in nothing" (James 1:2–4).

We can rejoice on two accounts. First, suffering provides a context for our faith to mature. The "trials of various kinds" represent the pressures of life that threaten our sense of well-being. When we are sick or stuck or grieved, we tend to doubt God's sovereignty and goodness in our lives. Every test of our body or mind or emotion is fundamentally a "testing of our faith" (1:3). In other words, the quality of our faith is proven in suffering, tested and shown to be genuine. In the way that an object is proven to be gold in the fire, the "proof" of our faith is in the "fiery trial" (1 Peter 4:12). Whether we are talking about common adversities or more acute hardships, we can embrace and even rejoice in suffering because we know that it produces character and hope and maturity (Romans 5:3, James 1:2–4).

Second, suffering focuses our hope on the consummation of all things, when God "will wipe away every tear from [our] eyes, and death shall be no more, neither shall there be mourning, nor crying, nor pain anymore" (Revelation 21:4). Just as Jesus endured the cross for the joy set before him (Hebrew 12:2), so too we look to the day when the steadfast will receive the crown of life (James 1:12). Indeed, "the sufferings of this present time are not worth comparing with the glory that is to be revealed to us" (Romans 8:18).

Wisdom, suffering, and maturity are all bound together in the person and work of Christ. He "became to us wisdom from God" (1 Corinthians 1:30), and he was made perfect through suffering (Hebrews 2:10). So then; we are justified by Christ's suffering and sanctified by ours. By this we are reminded that suffering is not a setback to our agendas, but rather an orientation to God's agenda, which is to form in us the character of Christ.

Ultimately, God does not ask us to explain suffering. He gives us his Spirit to comfort and strengthen us in our suffering. Even when we do not know how to pray, "the Spirit himself intercedes for us with groanings too deep for words" (Romans 8:26).

REFLECTION QUESTIONS
1. How has God used suffering in your life to mature your faith?
2. What fears do you have regarding suffering?
3. What promises of God speak to those fears?

CLOSING PRAYER

O God whose will conquers all, there is no comfort in anything apart from enjoying thee and being engaged in thy service. Thou art All in all, and all enjoyments are what to me thou makest them, and no more. I am well pleased with thy will, whatever it is, or should be in all respects, and if thou bidst me decide for myself in any affair, I would choose to refer all to thee, for thou art infinitely wise and cannot do amiss, as I am in danger of doing. I rejoice to think that all things are at thy disposal, and it delights me to leave them there. Then prayer turns wholly into praise, and all I can do is to adore and bless thee.[10]

---

[10] *The Valley of Vision*, 4.

Day 19

Daily Readings

CALL TO WORSHIP

Praise the LORD! Praise the name of the LORD, give praise, O servants of the LORD, who stand in the house of the LORD, in the courts of the house of our God! Praise the LORD, for the LORD is good; sing to his name, for it is pleasant! For the LORD has chosen Jacob for himself, Israel as his own possession. For I know that the LORD is great, and that our Lord is above all gods. Whatever the LORD pleases, he does, in heaven and on earth, in the seas and all deeps. Your name, O LORD, endures forever, your renown, O LORD, throughout all ages. For the LORD will vindicate his people and have compassion on his servants. O house of Levi, bless the LORD! You who fear the LORD, bless the LORD! Blessed be the LORD from Zion, he who dwells in Jerusalem! Praise the LORD!

Psalm 135:1–6, 13–14, 20–21

CONFESSION

O Christ, out of your fullness we have all received grace upon grace. You are our eternal hope; you are patient and full of mercy; you are generous to all who call upon you. Save us, Lord. O Christ, fountain of life and holiness, you have taken away our sins. On the cross you were wounded for our transgressions and were bruised for our iniquities. Save us, Lord. O Christ, obedient unto death, source of all comfort, our life and our resurrection, our peace and reconciliation: Save us, Lord. O Christ, Savior of all who trust you, hope of all who die for you, and joy of all the saints: Save us, Lord. Jesus, Lamb of God, have mercy on us. Jesus, bearer of our sins, have mercy on us. Jesus, redeemer of the world, grant us peace. Amen.[11]

GOSPEL OF MARK

And they sent to him some of the Pharisees and some of the Herodians, to trap him in his talk. And they came and said to him, "Teacher, we know that you are true and do not care about anyone's opinion. For you are not swayed by appearances, but truly teach the way of God. Is it lawful to pay taxes to Caesar, or not? Should we pay them, or should we not?" But, knowing their hypocrisy, he said to them, "Why put me to the test? Bring me a denarius and let me look at it." And they brought one. And he said to them, "Whose likeness and inscription is this?" They said to him, "Caesar's." Jesus said to them, "Render to Caesar the things that are Caesar's, and to God the things that are God's." And they marveled at him.

Mark 12:13–17

PRAYER OF THANKSGIVING

Lord God, the earth is yours along with everything in it. You are the Creator and Sustainer—to you is due all praise and honor and glory. Who are we that you are mindful of us? Who are we that you should set your seal of ownership upon us and put your Spirit inside us? Our lips shall speak of your praise!

Daily Devotion

And Jesus, full of the Holy Spirit, returned from the Jordan and was led by the Spirit in the wilderness for forty days, being tempted by the devil. And he ate nothing during those days. And when they were ended, he was hungry.

Luke 4:1–2

The forty days of Lent parallels the forty days that Jesus went without food in the wilderness. A common observance during this season is to deny ourselves of particular comforts and pleasures. The point is not to induce suffering, as if we could earn some kind of righteousness through

[11] *The Worship Sourcebook*, 562–563.

self-denial. <u>Our heart in Lent is simply to de-clutter</u> our self-absorbed lives, making room to remember how our Lord suffered for us.

The striking thing in this story is that Jesus went into the desert under the direction of the Holy Spirit. He chose this suffering. Indeed, his whole life was a choice to enter into our suffering. God does not tell us to go looking for suffering, but that does not mean he will always keep it from us. Jesus was in the wilderness because the Holy Spirit led him there. Further, the apostles were adamant that Jesus's death at the hands of sinners was "according to the definite plan and foreknowledge of God" (Acts 2:23). The testimony of Scripture is that <u>Christians need to embrace suffering</u> as part of our calling and endure it as part of our witness:

> » *"Beloved, <u>do not be surprised at the fiery trial when</u> it comes upon you to test you, as though something strange were happening to you" (1 Peter 4:12).*
> » *"For it has been granted to you that for the sake of Christ you should not only believe in hi<u>m but also suffer for his sake"</u> (Philippians 1:29).*
> » *"Indeed, all who desire to live a godly life in Christ Jesus will be <u>persecuted" (2 Timothy 3:12).</u>*

Our wilderness is not literal, but it is real. We are tempted to sustain ourselves, to escape our vulnerability, and to chase our aspirations without thought of others. But Jesus offers us another way, a humble way that waits patiently for the Spirit of God to direct our steps. He reveals to us what it means to embrace our humanity without shortcuts.

"The devil said to him, 'If you are the Son of God, command this stone to become bread'" (Luke 4:3). Certainly Jesus could have done this, but the lack of bread revealed a deeper hunger for God, and a deeper satisfaction of being sustained by God.

"And the devil took him up and showed him all the kingdoms of the world in a moment of time, and said to him . . . 'worship me, it will all be yours'" (4:5–7). It would all be his eventually, but to have it now would be to have it without suffering and death. How often do we worship whatever promises to give us what we want now, without inconvenience or discomfort? But Jesus worships God alone, not because it is easier, but because it is truer and far better.

"And [the devil] took him to Jerusalem and set him on the pinnacle of the temple and said to him, 'If you are the Son of God, throw yourself down from here, for it is written, "He will command his angels concerning you, to guard you"'" (4:9–10). Had Jesus done this, he could have ended all this temptation and trial. How often do we call upon God for miraculous solutions to our suffering, not because we trust him in our circumstance but because we want out of it? But Jesus would not put God to the test.

We live into our in-Christ-humanity by surrendering to the Holy Spirit, wherever he may lead us. This season is about waiting, maybe even suffering the loss of things that have come to define us, because we know that our life is dust, and because we are looking forward to resurrection life.

REFLECTION QUESTIONS

1. How does your inclination to avoid hardship hinder your ability to follow Jesus?
2. How does the Spirit's presence in your suffering comfort and strengthen you?
3. Is the Spirit currently leading you somewhere you don't want to go?

CLOSING PRAYER

O Holy Spirit, as the sun is full of light, the ocean full of water, Heaven full of glory, so may my heart be full of thee. Vain are all divine purposes of love and the redemption wrought by Jesus except thou work within, regenerating by thy power, giving me eyes to see Jesus, showing me the realities of the unseen world. Give me thyself without measure, as an unimpaired fountain, as inexhaustible riches.[12]

---

[12] *The Valley of Vision*, 50.

Day 20

Daily Readings

CALL TO WORSHIP

The law of the LORD is perfect, reviving the soul; the testimony of the LORD is sure, making wise the simple; the precepts of the LORD are right, rejoicing the heart; the commandment of the LORD is pure, enlightening the eyes; the fear of the LORD is clean, enduring forever; the rules of the LORD are true, and righteous altogether. More to be desired are they than gold, even much fine gold; sweeter also than honey and drippings of the honeycomb. Moreover, by them is your servant warned; in keeping them there is great reward.

Psalm 19:7–11

CONFESSION

Lord, you come to us, but we do not recognize you; you call, but we do not follow; you command, but we do not obey; you bless us, but we do not thank you. Please forgive and help us. Lord, you accept us, but we do not accept others; you forgive us, but we do not forgive those who wrong us; you love us, but we do not love our neighbors. Please forgive and help us. Lord, you showed us how to carry out your mission, but we still insist on our own; you identified with the poor and needy, but we seek our own wants and desires; you suffered and died for all, but we turn to our own comfort. In the midst of our lack of faith, you are always faithful! Please forgive and help us; you are the faithful one! Amen.[13]

---

[13] *The Worship Sourcebook*, 93.

GOSPEL OF MARK

And Sadducees came to him, who say that there is no resurrection. And they asked him a question, saying, "Teacher, Moses wrote for us that if a man's brother dies and leaves a wife, but leaves no child, the man must take the widow and raise up offspring for his brother. There were seven brothers; the first took a wife, and when he died left no offspring. And the second took her, and died, leaving no offspring. And the third likewise. And the seven left no offspring. Last of all the woman also died. In the resurrection, when they rise again, whose wife will she be? For the seven had her as wife." Jesus said to them, "Is this not the reason you are wrong, because you know neither the Scriptures nor the power of God? For when they rise from the dead, they neither marry nor are given in marriage, but are like angels in heaven. And as for the dead being raised, have you not read in the book of Moses, in the passage about the bush, how God spoke to him, saying, 'I am the God of Abraham, and the God of Isaac, and the God of Jacob'? He is not God of the dead, but of the living. You are quite wrong."

Mark 12:18–27

PRAYER OF THANKSGIVING

God of truth, your Word gives us life and light. In our legalism, your grace sustains us. In our license, your truth compels us. May the words of our mouth and the meditations of our heart be pleasing to you, O holy and merciful God.

Daily Devotion

My God, my God, why have you forsaken me? Why are you so far from saving me, from the words of my groaning?

Psalm 22:1

There are many prophecies in the Old Testament about the Messiah, some of which describe the suffering that he would endure. In Psalm 22, David's prayer reflects the anguish Jesus would experience in his death. Notice how accurately this foretells the words and experience of Jesus:

"My God, my God, why have you forsaken me? Why are you so far from saving me, from the words of my groaning? . . . But I am a worm and not a man, scorned by mankind and despised by the people. All who see me mock me; they make mouths at me; they wag their heads; 'He trusts in the LORD; let him deliver him; let him rescue him, for he delights in him!' . . . I am poured out like water, and all my bones are out of joint; my heart is like wax; it is melted within my breast; my strength is dried up like a potsherd, and my tongue sticks to my jaws; you lay me in the dust of death. For dogs encompass me; a company of evildoers encircles me; they have pierced my hands and feet—I can count all my bones—they stare and gloat over me; they divide my garments among them, and for my clothing they cast lots" (Psalm 22:1, 6–8, 14–18).

This psalm was written about six hundred years before Jesus was born. So when Jesus cried out on the cross, "My God, my God, why have you forsaken me?" he was revealing himself as the Messiah. But more than that, he cried out because the pain of abandonment was overwhelming. What he had tasted in the garden was now being poured out in its fullness upon the beloved Son.

Jesus suffered more than anyone has ever suffered. Even if we experienced the wrath of God against our sins, that would still not approach the degree of suffering that Jesus endured. He had never experienced sin or separation from God, yet he bore the entirety of his people's sin on the cross. No one has ever suffered like Jesus suffered.

We also see here that nobody has ever obeyed like Jesus obeyed. He turned to God even while he was being condemned. He was faithful even while being forsaken. No one has ever trusted and obeyed like this.

Jesus is described as a worm and not a man. This is an interesting metaphor in the context of persecution. When I am insulted or accused or mocked, my inclination is to defend myself. The human tendency is to be annoyed, envious, resentful, anxious, and proud. We are not like worms. We are more like a snake that rears up and strikes back. But Jesus was willing to let others tread on him. He did not strike back or defend himself. He went humbly and willingly to the cross.

Why did he do this? Because he had his mind set on something else.

Those who have their minds set on earthly things are, in Paul's words, "enemies of the cross of Christ" (Philippians 3:18). This phrase indicates that those who spurn suffering and make their primary aim comfort, success, and pleasure are at odds with the cross of Christ, the very symbol of his suffering. To shun our suffering is to shun his. To embrace his suffering is to embrace our own.

The reason suffering produces character and hope is because the Spirit uses our suffering to draw us deeper into relationship with God. This is why Paul's deepest desire was to know Christ and the power of his resurrection and the fellowship of sharing in his sufferings (3:10).

REFLECTION QUESTIONS

1. Have you ever felt abandoned or forsaken by God? Have you ever felt mocked or persecuted by others? Explain.
2. How might these experiences draw you deeper into a relationship with God?

CLOSING PRAYER

Strengthen me against temptations. My heart is an unexhausted fountain of sin, flowing on in every pattern of behaviour. Thou hast disarmed me of the means in which I trusted, and I have no strength but in thee. Thou alone canst hold back my evil ways, but without thy grace to sustain me I fall. Keep me sensible of my weakness, and of my dependence upon thy strength. Let every trial teach me more of thy peace, more of thy love. Thy Holy Spirit is given to increase thy graces, and I cannot preserve or improve them unless he works continually in me. May he confirm my trust in thy promised help, and let me walk humbly in dependence upon thee, for Jesus's sake.[14]

---

[14] *The Valley of Vision*, 310–311.

Day 21

Daily Readings

CALL TO WORSHIP

The earth is the LORD's and the fullness thereof, the world and those who dwell therein, for he has founded it upon the seas and established it upon the rivers. Who shall ascend the hill of the LORD? And who shall stand in his holy place? He who has clean hands and a pure heart, who does not lift up his soul to what is false and does not swear deceitfully. He will receive blessing from the LORD and righteousness from the God of his salvation. Such is the generation of those who seek him, who seek the face of the God of Jacob. Selah Lift up your heads, O gates! And be lifted up, O ancient doors, that the King of glory may come in. Who is this King of glory? The LORD, strong and mighty, the LORD, mighty in battle! Lift up your heads, O gates! And lift them up, O ancient doors, that the King of glory may come in. Who is this King of glory? The LORD of hosts, he is the King of glory!

Psalm 24

CONFESSION

Merciful God, we have not loved you with all our heart and mind and strength and soul. Lord, have mercy. We have not loved our neighbors as you have taught us. Christ, have mercy. We are indifferent to the saving grace of your Word and life. Lord, have mercy. Forgive and heal us by your steadfast love made known to us in the passion, death, and resurrection of Jesus Christ, our Lord. Amen.[15]

---

[15] *The Worship Sourcebook*, 597.

GOSPEL OF MARK

And one of the scribes came up and heard them disputing with one another, and seeing that he answered them well, asked him, "Which commandment is the most important of all?" Jesus answered, "The most important is, 'Hear, O Israel: The Lord our God, the Lord is one. And you shall love the Lord your God with all your heart and with all your soul and with all your mind and with all your strength.' The second is this: 'You shall love your neighbor as yourself.' There is no other commandment greater than these." And the scribe said to him, "You are right, Teacher. You have truly said that he is one, and there is no other besides him. And to love him with all the heart and with all the understanding and with all the strength, and to love one's neighbor as oneself, is much more than all whole burnt offerings and sacrifices." And when Jesus saw that he answered wisely, he said to him, "You are not far from the kingdom of God." And after that no one dared to ask him any more questions.

Mark 12:28–34

PRAYER OF THANKSGIVING

King of glory, you have set your steadfast love upon your people, and never removed it. You are faithful to your covenant people, unwavering in your promises. Holy and awesome is your name!

Daily Devotion

For to this you have been called, because Christ also suffered for you, leaving you an example, so that you might follow in his steps. He committed no sin, neither was deceit found in his mouth. When he was reviled, he did not revile in return; when he suffered, he did not threaten, but continued entrusting himself to him who judges justly. He himself bore our sins in his body on the tree, that we might die to sin and live to righteousness. By his wounds you have been healed.

1 Peter 2:21–24

In his letter to those who had been scattered because of persecution, Peter exhorts believers to look to the example of Christ in order to endure their suffering. Two themes are woven together here: the example of

Christ's suffering and the saving purpose of Christ's suffering. Since Jesus suffered for us, leaving us an example, belonging to him means following "in his steps" (2:21).

Peter's elaboration of Jesus's example clearly identifies him with the Suffering Servant of Isaiah 53, where the Messiah is portrayed not only as one who bears our sin on the cross, but also the one who carries the burden of sin to the cross. Just as the Suffering Servant "surely has borne our griefs and carried our sorrows" (Isaiah 53:4), Peter knew Jesus as one who grieved over sin and was burdened by the brokenness of the world (John 11:35, Luke 19:41). Just as the Suffering Servant was "oppressed, and he was afflicted, yet he opened not his mouth" (Isaiah 53:7), Peter recalls that, "when he was reviled, he did not revile in return; when he suffered, he did not threaten" (1 Peter 2:23).

The example of Christ was to endure accusation and insult without responding in kind. Instead, he "continued entrusting himself to him who judges justly" (2:23). Thus, Peter's exhortation is to "let those who suffer according to God's will entrust their souls to a faithful Creator while doing good" (4:19).

Peter not only saw Jesus as one who fulfilled the actions of the Suffering Servant, but also as the one sent by God to fulfill the purpose of the Suffering Servant. Edmund Clowney draws out both aspects when he writes, "In Isaiah's songs, the Servant is both identified with the people of God and distinguished from them. He suffers for them, stands in their place, and bears the judgment of their sins."[16]

That Jesus "committed no sin" (1 Peter 2:22) and yet was crucified speaks to the injustice of his death, humanly speaking. However, Peter would have remembered that on the day when Jesus the innocent was sentenced to death, Barabbas the insurrectionist was set free (Mark 15:15). We are like Barabbas, guilty and deserving of death, but set free through the "unjust" substitution of Jesus in our place. This is the just justification of God: "the righteous for the unrighteous" (1 Peter 3:18).

---

[16] Edmund Clowney, *The Message of 1 Peter*, The Bible Speaks Today Series, ed. John W. Stott (Downers Grove: InterVaristy Press, 1988), 119.

In whatever suffering or persecution comes our way, we are to follow in Jesus's steps. For Peter, Jesus's suffering was not merely an example, for apart from the saving purpose of Christ's suffering, the example is of little value. The purpose of his suffering was to bear "our sins in his body on the tree, that we might die to sin and live to righteousness" (1 Peter 2:24). We can endure suffering because Jesus suffered for us. We have hope because we have been healed.

REFLECTION QUESTIONS

1. How does Jesus's life challenge your view of suffering?
2. How does his death move you?

CLOSING PRAYER

Blessed Lord Jesus, no human mind could conceive or invent the gospel. Acting in eternal grace, you are both its messenger and its message, lived out on earth through infinite compassion, applying your life to insult, injury, death, that I might be redeemed, ransomed, freed. Blessed be you, O Father, for contriving this way; eternal thanks to you, O Lamb of God, for opening this way, praise everlasting to you, O Holy Spirit, for applying this way to my heart. Glorious Trinity, impress the gospel upon my soul, until its virtue diffuses every faculty. Let it be heard, acknowledged, professed, felt. O unite me to yourself with inseparable bonds, that nothing may ever draw me back from you, my Lord, my Saviour.[1]

---

[1] *The Valley of Vision*, 62–63.

Day 22

Daily Readings

CALL TO WORSHIP

And now, Israel, what does the LORD your God require of you, but to fear the LORD your God, to walk in all his ways, to love him, to serve the LORD your God with all your heart and with all your soul, and to keep the commandments and statutes of the LORD, which I am commanding you today for your good? Behold, to the LORD your God belong heaven and the heaven of heavens, the earth with all that is in it. Yet the LORD set his heart in love on your fathers and chose their offspring after them, you above all peoples, as you are this day. Circumcise therefore the foreskin of your heart, and be no longer stubborn. For the LORD your God is God of gods and Lord of lords, the great, the mighty, and the awesome God, who is not partial and takes no bribe. He executes justice for the fatherless and the widow, and loves the sojourner, giving him food and clothing. Love the sojourner, therefore, for you were sojourners in the land of Egypt. You shall fear the LORD your God. You shall serve him and hold fast to him, and by his name you shall swear. He is your praise. He is your God, who has done for you these great and terrifying things that your eyes have seen. Your fathers went down to Egypt seventy persons, and now the LORD your God has made you as numerous as the stars of heaven.

Deuteronomy 10:12–22

CONFESSION

Almighty and merciful God, we confess to you that too often we approach you out of duty and obligation rather than genuine love and affection for your presence. Forgive us for uttering songs of praise to you without being transformed by the truths that we are singing. Forgive us for muttering prayers of adoration to you without depending upon your love and grace. And forgive us for acting as though you are pleased with our show, pretense, and religious activities, when we do not love our neighbor. You take no pleasure in these worthless offerings, they are an abomination to you. You will hide your eyes from us, and you will not listen. We confess that we seek comfort and isolation rather than moving toward people, like you have moved toward us. We humbly ask that you would teach us to do what is truly good; that we would seek justice and correct oppression. We pray that we would love seeing things made right in this world because you have first made us right through the cross of Christ. Amen. (Based on Isaiah 1:10–17.)

GOSPEL OF MARK

And as Jesus taught in the temple, he said, "How can the scribes say that the Christ is the son of David? David himself, in the Holy Spirit, declared, "'The Lord said to my Lord, "Sit at my right hand, until I put your enemies under your feet."' David himself calls him Lord. So how is he his son?" And the great throng heard him gladly. And in his teaching he said, "Beware of the scribes, who like to walk around in long robes and like greetings in the marketplaces and have the best seats in the synagogues and the places of honor at feasts, who devour widows' houses and for a pretense make long prayers. They will receive the greater condemnation."

Mark 12:35–40

PRAYER OF THANKSGIVING

We praise you God, that in Christ, there is no condemnation. Through his blood we have been washed clean of our sin. Through his perfect offering and sacrifice, we have been forgiven of our hypocrisy and made right. Thanks be to the Spirit, who has set us free in Christ from the law of sin and death.

Daily Devotion

> Yet another said, "I will follow you, Lord, but let me first say farewell to those at my home." Jesus said to him, "No one who puts his hand to the plow and looks back is fit for the kingdom of God."
>
> Luke 9:61–62

During Lent we give extended thought to the suffering that Jesus endured, but we know the outcome—an empty tomb. For us, this is an exercise in reflection, but for the disciples it was a testing of faith. We see what God was doing in the garden of Gethsemane, and we know the great necessity of the cross of Christ. Otherwise, we too would fall asleep and run for safety. It's easy to look back.

Jesus saw it coming. Luke says, "When the days drew near for him to be taken up, he set his face to go to Jerusalem" (Luke 9:51). Knowing what had to happen, Jesus stayed the course. A serious reflection on his suffering must account for the fact that our Lord looked forward, never back. He was honest about the implications of this reality for any who would follow him (Luke 9:62)

We look back all the time, longing for comforts past, wondering what might have been. Even though we have taken up life with Jesus, seasons of suffering challenge our resolve and fix our attention to how things used to be. Our hunger for restoration and relief from burdens turns our heart to the past, but Jesus has only an eye for what is set before him.

The Israelites experienced this in the forty years they spent wandering in the desert. They argued with Moses, idealized their life in Egypt, and questioned the goodness of the Lord. They complained about the Lord's provision, not because he didn't provide, but because they weren't content with what he provided.

The paradox of suffering is that it is actually a gift—one we might like at times to give back—but a gift nonetheless. God gives us suffering as a way of giving us himself, for it is in our suffering that we become acutely aware of his presence and power. Hardship empties us of our self-reliance so that we might walk in the Spirit, who "bears witness with our spirit that we are children of God, and if children, then heirs—heirs of God and fellow heirs with Christ, provided we suffer with him in order that we may also be glorified with him" (Romans 8:16–17).

The Israelites in the wilderness and Christ on the cross both stand as a testament that God does not forsake his people. More than this, they remind us that suffering is a gift from God that tangibly embeds his promises in our daily life. Of course, we have to be looking to him to receive it as such.

Ultimately, suffering is about learning to receive whatever God has placed in our hands as his goodness for us today. For Jesus, the journey to cross was a gift. Gethsemane and Golgotha were gifts. They were not easy gifts to receive, which is why he had to say, "Not what I will, but what you will" (Mark 14:36), and why he taught us to pray, "Your kingdom come, your will be done" (Matthew 6:10), because if we are not looking for God's kingdom come, we always be looking back for our kingdom gone.

REFLECTION QUESTIONS

1. What do you long for from the past?
2. How can you see God's goodness in your present hardships?
3. What do you need from God to move forward in faith?

CLOSING PRAYER

Fill me with thy Spirit that I may be occupied with his presence. May his comforts cheer me in my sorrows, his strength sustain me in my trials, his blessings revive me in my weariness, his presence render me a fruitful tree of holiness, his might establish me in peace and joy, his incitements make me ceaseless in prayer, his animation kindle in me undying devotion. Send him as the searcher of my heart, to show me more of my corruptions and helplessness that I may flee to thee, cling to thee, rest on thee, as the beginning and end of my salvation.[2]

---

[2] *The Valley of Vision*, 54–55.

FOURTH SUNDAY OF LENT

In life and in death we belong to God. Through the grace of our Lord Jesus Christ, the love of God, and the communion of the Holy Spirit, we trust in the one triune God, the Holy One of Israel, whom alone we worship and serve. We trust in Jesus Christ, fully human, fully God. Jesus proclaimed the reign of God: preaching good news to the poor and release to the captives, forgiving sinners, and calling all to repent and believe the gospel. Unjustly condemned for blasphemy and sedition, Jesus was crucified, suffering the depths of human pain and giving his life for the sins of the world. God raised Jesus from the dead, vindicating his sinless life, breaking the power of sin and evil, delivering us from death to life eternal. With believers in every time and place, we rejoice that nothing in life or in death can separate us from the love of God in Christ Jesus, our Lord. Glory be to the Father, and to the Son, and to the Holy Spirit. Amen.[3]

Hallelujah unto Jesus!
Now He lives to die no more;
Let all nations sing His praises,
Gladly sing them o'er and o'er.

Hallelujah! Hallelujah!
Hallelujah! to our king!
From the tomb today He's risen,
Hallelujah we'll sing.

Hallelujah unto Jesus!
Who for us once bled, and died,
He is now o'er death, the victor,
Hail Him king the Crucified.

Hallelujah unto Jesus!
Blessed firstfruits of the dead;
He our resurrection surety,
Lives for us our risen king.

---

[3] A Brief Statement of Faith, 1991, Office of the General Assembly, Presbyterian Church (USA).

Hallelujah unto Jesus!
Death is robbed now of its sting;
And the tomb for us is lighted,
Hallelujah to our king.[4]

---

[4] Mary M. Kennedy, "Hallelujah Unto Jesus," 1903.

WEEK FOUR: LAMENT

Day 23

Daily Readings

CALL TO WORSHIP

I will bless the LORD at all times; his praise shall continually be in my mouth. My soul makes its boast in the LORD; let the humble hear and be glad. Oh, magnify the LORD with me, and let us exalt his name together! I sought the LORD, and he answered me and delivered me from all my fears. Those who look to him are radiant, and their faces shall never be ashamed. This poor man cried, and the LORD heard him and saved him out of all his troubles. The angel of the LORD encamps around those who fear him, and delivers them. Oh, taste and see that the LORD is good! Blessed is the man who takes refuge in him! Oh, fear the LORD, you his saints, for those who fear him have no lack! . . . The LORD is near to the brokenhearted and saves the crushed in spirit.

Psalm 34:1–9, 18

CONFESSION

Gracious God, we affirm that you alone are good. But we have sought our good in other things. We have pursued joy in the creation rather than in the Creator. We have not loved what is truly good. Forgive our sin, O God. Forgive us for refusing to believe that you are good, and that you do good. Have mercy upon us, according to your goodness, according to your unfailing love. Amen.

GOSPEL OF MARK

And he sat down opposite the treasury and watched the people putting money into the offering box. Many rich people put in large sums. And a poor widow came and put in two small copper coins, which make a penny. And he called his disciples to him and said to them, "Truly, I say to you, this poor widow has put in more than all those who are contributing to the offering box. For they all contributed out of their abundance, but she out of her poverty has put in everything she had, all she had to live on."

Mark 12:41–44

PRAYER OF THANKSGIVING

We praise you God that you are good and that you work for our good. Every good and perfect gift is from you. You do not change and you never fail. Thanks be to God!

Daily Devotion

The LORD is near to the brokenhearted and saves the crushed in spirit.

Psalm 34:18

Lent is a season of sorrow. It reminds us of the frail and fallen condition of our world, and certainly in our own body and soul. Our reflections during this season stir a deep sense that something is wrong. Something greater than just our individual sin, it is the pervasive effects of sin. Distraction. Deception. Discord. Despair. Disaster. Death. These are deep wounds.

What are we supposed to do with our pain, anger, grief, and confusion? Can I bring these things before God? People like Job, David, Jeremiah, and even Jesus reveal to us that these emotions can be turned into prayers of faith.

First, hear the good news: "The LORD is near to the brokenhearted and saves the crushed in spirit" (Psalm 34:18). Not only does God hear and understand our pain, he is especially inclined toward those who are hurting. We often think that being a Christian means we must always be happy, sweeping our grief under the rug of God's sovereignty. Yet, God desires to enter into our pain: "The Spirit helps us in our weakness. For we do not know what to pray for as we ought, but the Spirit himself intercedes for us with groanings too deep for words" (Romans 8:26).

Second, the Scriptures teach us to lament, to wail and mourn and plead before the God who draws near to the brokenhearted.

> » *Jeremiah lamented over the plight of Israel because of her sin: "All her people groan as they search for bread; they trade their treasures for food to revive their strength. 'Look, O LORD, and see, for I am despised. . . . For these things I weep; my eyes flow with tears; for a comforter is far from me, one to revive my spirit; my children are desolate, or the enemy has prevailed'" (Lamentations 1:11,16).*
>
> » *The psalmists lamented in times of trouble: "With my voice I cry out to the LORD; with my voice I plead for mercy to the LORD. I pour out my complaint before him; I tell my trouble before him" (Psalm 142:1–2).*
>
> » *Jesus lamented over Jerusalem: "O Jerusalem, Jerusalem, the city that kills the prophets and stones those who are sent to it! How often would I have gathered your children together as a hen gathers her brood under her wings, and you were not willing!" (Matthew 23:37).*

Lament is not about getting things off your chest. It's about casting your anxieties upon God, and trusting him with them. Mere complaining indicates a lack of intimacy with God. Because lament is a form of prayer, it transforms our complaints into worship.

Anyone can complain; Christians can lament. They can talk to God about their condition and ask him to change things because they have a relationship with him. To lament is to be utterly honest with God because we trust him.

Biblical lament affirms that suffering is real and spiritually significant, but not hopeless. In his mercy, our God has given us a form of language that bends his ear and pulls his heart.

REFLECTION QUESTIONS

1. What are you angered or grieved by—in your life or in the world around you?

2.   How do you normally deal with these emotions? Write a prayer of lament to God, asking him for help and relief.

CLOSING PRAYER

We hear Jesus say: "My God, my God, why have you forsaken me?" And we too at times pray: "Why are you so far from helping me, from the words of my groaning? O my God, I cry by day, but you do not answer; and by night, but find no rest. Yet you are holy, enthroned on the praises of Israel. In you our ancestors trusted; they trusted, and you delivered them. To you they cried and were saved; in you they trusted and were not put to shame." We hear the words of the ancient psalm even as we see Jesus: "But I am a worm and not human; scorned by others, and despised by the people. All who see me mock at me; they make mouths at me, they shake their heads; 'Commit your cause to the LORD; let him deliver—let him rescue the one in whom he delights!'" And we too pray: "Yet it was you who took me from the womb; you kept me safe on my mother's breast. On you I was cast from my birth, and since my mother bore me you have been my God. Do not be far from me, for trouble is near and there is no one to help."[5]

---

[5] *The Worship Sourcebook*, 611.

Day 24

Daily Readings

CALL TO WORSHIP

Come and hear, all you who fear God, and I will tell what he has done for my soul. I cried to him with my mouth, and high praise was on my tongue. If I had cherished iniquity in my heart, the Lord would not have listened. But truly God has listened; he has attended to the voice of my prayer. Blessed be God, because he has not rejected my prayer or removed his steadfast love from me!

Psalm 66:16–20

CONFESSION

O Lord, do not rebuke us in your anger or discipline us in your wrath. For your arrows have pierced us, and your hand has come down upon us. Our bodies waste away because of our sin; our guilt overwhelms us. We confess our iniquity; we are troubled by our sin. O Lord, do not forsake us; be not far from us, O God. Forgive our sin, and make us new, that we might have peace with you, peace with each other, and peace within ourselves.

GOSPEL OF MARK

And as he came out of the temple, one of his disciples said to him, "Look, Teacher, what wonderful stones and what wonderful buildings!" And Jesus said to him, "Do you see these great buildings? There will not be left here one stone upon another that will not be thrown down." And as he sat on the Mount of Olives opposite the temple, Peter and James and John and Andrew asked him privately,

"Tell us, when will these things be, and what will be the sign when all these things are about to be accomplished?" And Jesus began to say to them, "See that no one leads you astray. Many will come in my name, saying, 'I am he!' and they will lead many astray. And when you hear of wars and rumors of wars, do not be alarmed. This must take place, but the end is not yet. For nation will rise against nation, and kingdom against kingdom. There will be earthquakes in various places; there will be famines. These are but the beginning of the birth pains."

Mark 13:1–8

PRAYER OF THANKSGIVING

Thank you God for not rejecting our prayers or removing your love from us. Thank you for listening and hearing us when we cry to you. Thank you for attending to our voice and drawing near in our weakness.

Daily Devotion

How long, O LORD? Will you forget me forever? How long will you hide your face from me? How long must I take counsel in my soul and have sorrow in my heart all the day? How long shall my enemy be exalted over me? Consider and answer me, O LORD my God; light up my eyes, lest I sleep the sleep of death, lest my enemy say, "I have prevailed over him," lest my foes rejoice because I am shaken. But I have trusted in your steadfast love; my heart shall rejoice in your salvation. I will sing to the LORD, because he has dealt bountifully with me.

Psalm 13

The best way to learn the language of lament is to enter into the prayers made available to us. These are intimate windows into the human soul and the heart of God. Let's consider Psalm 13, a lament of King David.

David is at the end of his rope. He is tired of trying, almost to the point of despair. In the midst of his physical and emotional fatigue, he cries out to the Lord: "How long, O LORD?" (13:1).

How often have we wanted to ask this very question: "How long! How long must I carry around this burden, how long will the helpless be oppressed, how long will injustice run wild, how long will racism divide us, how long will sickness wreck our bodies?" We have asked these questions with wet cheeks and clenched fists, but have we directed our cry to God?

David wonders if God has removed his hand from his life, but his words are decidedly addressed to God: "Consider and answer me, O LORD my God; light up my eyes, lest I sleep the sleep of death" (13:3). He is not just venting. He wants answers. He wants to see a light at the end of the tunnel, the light of God's presence, the light of justice. Anything else feels like death.

What hope does he have of being delivered from his sorrow into the light of God's presence? What reason does he have to believe that God will bridge the divide and answer his cry for help? He leans not on his present experience of God, but rather the eternal character of God: "But I have trusted in your steadfast love; my heart shall rejoice in your salvation" (13:5).

The Hebrew word for steadfast love is *hesed*, a rich, complex word that means so much more than what we often mean when we say *love*.

I love my wife, and I love coconut in my chili. You know there is a difference, of course, but you have to infer the meaning based on the context. Spousal love is much different than love of food. Even when I do not have warm, fuzzy feelings for my wife—hypothetically speaking—I am still committed to her in a way that I am not committed to anyone or anything else. And my loyal love flows from that commitment.

If you take away the context, then it's easy to reduce love to something that is basically sentimental, which is how many people think of God's love. Most people would say that God is a loving God, but their notion of God's love lacks substance because it has been removed from the context of redemptive history, wherein his mighty deeds toward his people flow from his covenantal commitment to them.

The hesed of God is a combination of strength in action, fierce commitment, and tender emotional care. God is a mighty warrior, a faithful husband, and a wise Father. This is the love that David remembers and trusts in his time of need. This is how he can begin with "How long?" (13:1), and end with "my heart shall rejoice" (13:5).

The goal of deliverance is always worship. May the love of God, "poured into our hearts through the Holy Spirit" (Romans 5:5) fill us up and turn our complaints into a song of praise.

REFLECTION QUESTIONS

1. What are your "how long?" questions?
2. How have you experienced God's love in the past?
3. How do you need to grow in your understanding of God's love in order to trust him now?

CLOSING PRAYER

Remembering Jesus, we make bold even in our lament to offer words of trust and praise: "I will tell of your name to my brothers and sisters; in the midst of the congregation I will praise you: You who fear the LORD, praise him! All you offspring of Jacob, glorify him; stand in awe of him, all you offspring of Israel! For he did not despise or abhor the affliction of the afflicted; he did not hide his face from me, but heard when I cried to him. From you comes my praise in the great congregation; my vows I will pay before those who fear him. The poor shall eat and be satisfied; those who seek him shall praise the LORD. May your hearts live forever! All the ends of the earth shall remember and turn to the LORD; and all the families of the nations shall worship before him. For dominion belongs to the LORD, and he rules over the nations. To him, indeed, shall all who sleep in the earth bow down; before him shall bow all who go down to the dust, and I shall live for him. Posterity will serve him; future generations will be told about the Lord, and proclaim his deliverance to a people yet unborn, saying that he has done it."[6]

---

[6] *The Worship Sourcebook*, 612.

Day 25

Daily Readings

CALL TO WORSHIP

> But this I call to mind, and therefore I have hope: The steadfast love of the LORD never ceases; his mercies never come to an end; they are new every morning; great is your faithfulness. "The LORD is my portion," says my soul, "therefore I will hope in him." The LORD is good to those who wait for him, to the soul who seeks him. It is good that one should wait quietly for the salvation of the LORD.
>
> Lamentations 3:21–26

CONFESSION

We are a forgetful people, O Lord. We have not cherished your Word in our hearts. We have not walked in its light. In our fear, we have doubted your goodness, and sought our own will above yours. We have chased after our own desires, thinking they will satisfy us. But we are brought low by our sins. Forgive us, O Lord. Cover our shame and deliver us from our iniquity. Our flesh and our heart may fail, but you are the strength of our heart and our portion forever.

GOSPEL OF MARK

> But be on your guard. For they will deliver you over to councils, and you will be beaten in synagogues, and you will stand before governors and kings for my sake, to bear witness before them. And the gospel must first be proclaimed to all nations. And when they bring you to trial and deliver you over, do not be anxious beforehand what you are to say, but say whatever is given you in that hour, for it is not you who

speak, but the Holy Spirit. And brother will deliver brother over to death, and the father his child, and children will rise against parents and have them put to death. And you will be hated by all for my name's sake. But the one who endures to the end will be saved.

Mark 13:9–13

PRAYER OF THANKSGIVING

Father of mercies, great is your steadfast love and faithfulness. Out of your goodness you have provided all that we have needed. You are our portion, now and forevermore.

Daily Devotion

> My eyes will flow without ceasing, without respite, until the LORD from heaven looks down and sees; my eyes cause me grief at the fate of all the daughters of my city.

Lamentations 3:49–51

Perhaps the most notable lamenter in all of Scripture is Jeremiah, also known as the "weeping prophet." As a prophet and a priest, he lived in the tension of representing God and the people. The people were unfaithful to God, and would not listen to the prophet's warning. He longed for them to repent, but he could see the judgment of God coming. There would be no deliverance, only captivity and exile.

The book of Lamentations captures the pain and prayer that are bound up in the heart of the one who weeps for his beloved city. In the first chapter, we see the plight of Jerusalem. She has been ransacked, and left desolate in shame. Her people have been enslaved by the enemy. They are reaping the destruction of the sins they had sown. Jeremiah knows it is just, but he is also one of them: "You have brought the day you announced; now let them be as I am. . . . for my groans are many, and my heart is faint" (1:21–22).

It is an honest view of things. The futility of creation and the injustice of our world are ultimately products of the fall. We are products of the fall, and some of our suffering is the Lord's discipline. Our sin is ever before us, and we cannot say we deserve to be spared.

In the second chapter of Lamentations, "The Lord has become like an enemy. . . . he has multiplied in the daughter of Judah mourning and lamentation" (2:5).

The apostle Paul asked the rhetorical question: "If God is for us, who can be against us?" (Romans 8:31). But what about when it feels like God is against us? Then who could be for us, and how could it possibly matter? It is an unbearable thought, one that prompted Jeremiah to question God: "With whom have you dealt thus?" (2:20). In other words, why must we suffer as no one has ever suffered?

In chapter three, Jeremiah has lost all hope. The fount of words and tears is bone dry (3:16–18). But then, "having poured all of himself out in lament, he finds in his emptiness a greater hope than he could have imagined: the surprising hope of *hesed*."[7] Cherish this oasis in the wilderness of Lamentations: "But this I call to mind, and therefore I have hope: The steadfast love of the LORD never ceases; his mercies never come to an end; they are new every morning; great is your faithfulness. 'The LORD is my portion,' says my soul, 'therefore I will hope in him.' The LORD is good to those who wait for him, to the soul who seeks him" (3:20–25). None of us would choose exile, but Jeremiah says, "It is good that one should wait quietly for the salvation of the LORD" (3:26).

Lent is a season of waiting, and it is hard to engage these heavy themes week after week. We are not accustomed to this kind of burden. Our soul is impatient for Easter, but Jeremiah says we need to sit in our lament for a while. Waiting, even when we don't feel God's presence, has a way of teaching us this important truth: "The Lord will not cast off forever, but, though he cause grief, he will have compassion according to the abundance of his steadfast love; for he does not afflict from his heart or grieve the children of men" (3:31–33).

We must learn this firsthand, so that we will "not regard lightly the discipline of the Lord, nor be weary when reproved by him. For the Lord disciplines the one he loves, and chastises every son whom he receives" (Hebrews 12:5–6).

---

[7] Michael Card, *A Sacred Sorrow: Reaching Out to God in the Lost Language of Lament (Quiet Times for the Heart)* (Colorado Springs: NavPress, 1995), 95.

REFLECTION QUESTIONS

1. What are you waiting for?
2. How is God using that to draw you near to himself?

CLOSING PRAYER

Where are you, O God? We are lost in the night; have you cast us from your presence? Temptations surround us; their masks grin through the darkness. We run from them, but which way should we go? Where can we hide when all lies in shadow? Have mercy on us, O God. Our eyes are swollen from tears; our bones are cold with fear; our souls have been broken—do you not hear, Lord? Save us! According to your steadfast love, answer us! Do not hide your face, but draw near and redeem us![8]

---

[8] *The Worship Sourcebook*, 568.

Day 26

Daily Readings

CALL TO WORSHIP

Oh give thanks to the LORD, for he is good, for his steadfast love endures forever! Let the redeemed of the LORD say so, whom he has redeemed from trouble and gathered in from the lands, from the east and from the west, from the north and from the south. Some wandered in desert wastes, finding no way to a city to dwell in; hungry and thirsty, their soul fainted within them. Then they cried to the LORD in their trouble, and he delivered them from their distress. He led them by a straight way till they reached a city to dwell in. Let them thank the LORD for his steadfast love, for his wondrous works to the children of man! For he satisfies the longing soul, and the hungry soul he fills with good things. Let them thank the LORD for his steadfast love, for his wondrous works to the children of man!

Psalm 107:1–9, 15

CONFESSION

O Lord, we confess our hands are not clean, our hearts are not pure. Forgive our capricious discipleship and keep our faith constant, O Lord. Lead us always to a deeper experience of your love. Enliven us by the familiar, but always new, story of shame and triumph, suffering and hope, that this Lenten journey reveals. Mold us to the ways of the Servant whose life we honor. In the name of Christ, our Lord, Amen.[9]

---

[9] *The Worship Sourcebook*, 586–587.

GOSPEL OF MARK

But when you see the abomination of desolation standing where he ought not to be, then let those who are in Judea flee to the mountains. Let the one who is on the housetop not go down, nor enter his house, to take anything out, and let the one who is in the field not turn back to take his cloak. And alas for women who are pregnant and for those who are nursing infants in those days! Pray that it may not happen in winter. For in those days there will be such tribulation as has not been from the beginning of the creation that God created until now, and never will be. And if the Lord had not cut short the days, no human being would be saved. But for the sake of the elect, whom he chose, he shortened the days. And then if anyone says to you, "Look, here is the Christ!" or "Look, there he is!" do not believe it. For false christs and false prophets will arise and perform signs and wonders, to lead astray, if possible, the elect. But be on guard; I have told you all things beforehand.

Mark 13:14–23

PRAYER OF THANKSGIVING

God of grace, through our union with Jesus, you have blessed us by giving us every spiritual blessing in the heavenly places. You chose us through our union with Christ, so that we would be holy and without fault before him. We thank you for the riches of your grace.

Daily Devotion

Therefore, brothers, since we have confidence to enter the holy places by the blood of Jesus, by the new and living way that he opened for us through the curtain, that is, through his flesh, and since we have a great priest over the house of God, let us draw near with a true heart in full assurance of faith, with our hearts sprinkled clean from an evil conscience and our bodies washed with pure water.

Hebrews 10:19–22

As Jeremiah laments over the condition of his people, he is revived by the remembrance of God's hesed (Lamentations 3:21–22). His situation has not changed, but his outlook has. God will show up eventually, because that is what he does. He cannot deny himself. He will not forsake his people.

Having seen the light of God's mercy, Jeremiah turns his eye back to the desolate city. It is a pile of ashes where once a glorious fire was ablaze. Those who never gave a second thought to their next meal are stealing from the mouths of children. The wealthy are impoverished, the beautiful disfigured, and the compassionate show no mercy.

The final chapter is an extended plea for the Lord to "remember what has befallen us," to "look, and see our disgrace!" (Lamentations 5:1).[10] It is not that God has forgotten or is unaware. Memory is not the issue, but rather presence and power. Jeremiah is asking the Lord to look and see their plight in hope that he will do something about it.

Recall Israel's captivity in Egypt: "During those many days the king of Egypt died, and the people of Israel groaned because of their slavery and cried out for help. Their cry for rescue from slavery came up to God. And God heard their groaning, and God remembered his covenant with Abraham, with Isaac, and with Jacob. God saw the people of Israel—and God knew" (Exodus 2:23–25). God knew what he had to do, because he remembered what he had promised to do.

This is some of what Jeremiah asks God to remember: They are like orphans and widows (5:3); they have become weary slaves (vs. 4–8); people are killing for food (vs. 9–10); women are being raped (v. 11); their leaders have been removed (vs. 12,14); the joys of life are a distant memory (vs. 13, 15); their city is in ruins (v. 18). Provocative imagery, vivid language, and passionate expression: this is the language of love and lament, of prophet and priest.

Jeremiah was torn between his love for his own people and his commitment to his God, and could do nothing but fill that abyss with his tears. Jeremiah points us to our ultimate hope, the great Prophet and High Priest, Christ Jesus our Lord. When Jesus stood in that awful gap between God and his people, the curtain of the temple was torn asunder. The presence and power of God was made available to all who

---

[10] Card, 97.

would come in faith. Their mourning would be turned into laughing. Come, "let us draw near with a true heart in full assurance of faith" (Hebrews 10:22).

REFLECTION QUESTIONS

1. What do you want the Lord to "look and see" in your life, in your town, and in our world?
2. What promises do you want to remind him of?

CLOSING PRAYER

My God, my God, why have you forsaken me? Why are you so far from saving me, from the words of my groaning? O my God, I cry by day, but you do not answer, and by night, but I find no rest. Yet you are holy, enthroned on the praises of Israel. In you our fathers trusted; they trusted, and you delivered them. To you they cried and were rescued; in you they trusted and were not put to shame. All the ends of the earth shall remember and turn to the LORD, and all the families of the nations shall worship before you. For kingship belongs to the LORD, and he rules over the nations.

Psalm 22:1–5, 27–28

Day 27

Daily Readings

CALL TO WORSHIP

God is our refuge and strength, a very present help in trouble. Therefore we will not fear though the earth gives way, though the mountains be moved into the heart of the sea, though its waters roar and foam, though the mountains tremble at its swelling. There is a river whose streams make glad the city of God, the holy habitation of the Most High. God is in the midst of her; she shall not be moved; God will help her when morning dawns. The nations rage, the kingdoms totter; he utters his voice, the earth melts. The LORD of hosts is with us; the God of Jacob is our fortress. Come, behold the works of the LORD, how he has brought desolations on the earth. He makes wars cease to the end of the earth; he breaks the bow and shatters the spear; he burns the chariots with fire. "Be still, and know that I am God. I will be exalted among the nations, I will be exalted in the earth!" The LORD of hosts is with us; the God of Jacob is our fortress.

Psalm 46

CONFESSION

Almighty and merciful God, we have erred and strayed from your ways like lost sheep. We have followed too much the devices and desires of our own hearts. We have offended against your holy laws. We have left undone those things which we ought to have done; and we have done those things which we ought not to have done. O Lord, have mercy upon us. Spare those who confess their faults. Restore those who are penitent, according to your promises declared to the world in your son. And grant, O merciful God, that we may live in your light and walk in your ways for the sake of Jesus Christ, our Savior. Amen.[11]

GOSPEL OF MARK

But in those days, after that tribulation, the sun will be darkened, and the moon will not give its light, and the stars will be falling from heaven, and the powers in the heavens will be shaken. And then they will see the Son of Man coming in clouds with great power and glory. And then he will send out the angels and gather his elect from the four winds, from the ends of the earth to the ends of heaven. From the fig tree learn its lesson: as soon as its branch becomes tender and puts out its leaves, you know that summer is near. So also, when you see these things taking place, you know that he is near, at the very gates. Truly, I say to you, this generation will not pass away until all these things take place. Heaven and earth will pass away, but my words will not pass away.

Mark 13:24–31

PRAYER OF THANKSGIVING

Most High God, who is present with us in all things, we take refuge in your strength. Before you we do not need to hide or prove ourselves in any way. Before you we can be still and rest in your power and goodness. Our heavenly Father is our hope, Christ is our Shepherd and Guardian, the Holy Spirit is our shelter. Amen.

Daily Devotion

It is better to go to a house of mourning than to go to a house of feasting, for death is the destiny of every man; the living should take this to heart. Sorrow is better than laughter, because a sad face is good for the heart. The heart of the wise is in the house of mourning, but the heart of fools is in the house of pleasure.

Ecclesiastes 7:2–4

On any given Sunday, we worship next to people who are struggling. They are going through the motions of the service, but inside they are

---

[11] *The Worship Sourcebook*, 90.

confused or hurting or even angry with God. The music is upbeat. The message is well meant, but all of that does not address the depth of loss they feel.

It is one thing to lament in the privacy of our own home or mind, but it takes a different kind of courage and faith to lament with and for another. Michael Card comments, "We're afraid of other people's pain. Like Job's friends, we're afraid when we don't have answers. Job doesn't get any answers for his sufferings, but he gets God."[12] To enter into someone's suffering, and to lament with them, is to seek God with them.

Sadly, Card is right. We are uneasy with pain and sorrow. In the forward to Card's book, Eugene Peterson asks the question: "Why are Christians, of all people, embarrassed by tears, uneasy in the presence of sorrow, unpracticed in the language of lament? It certainly is not a biblical heritage, for virtually all our ancestors in the faith were thoroughly 'acquainted with grief.' And our Savior was, as everyone knows, 'a Man of Sorrows.'"[13]

Peterson's answer: "At least one reason why people are uncomfortable with tears and the sight of suffering is that it is a blasphemous assault on their precariously maintained American spirituality of the pursuit of happiness. They want to avoid evidence that things are not right with the world as it is— without Jesus (and Job, David, and Jeremiah), without love, without faith, without sacrifice. It is a lot easier to keep the American faith if they don't have to look into the face of suffering, if they don't have to listen to our laments, if they don't have to deal with our tears."[14]

Much of contemporary Christianity has sought to insulate itself from the real, broken world. If we're not careful, we'll lose touch with reality. This is why King Solomon says, "It is better to go to the house of mourning than to go to the house of feasting" (Ecclesiastes 7:2).

---

[12] "Calvin College." *Bringing Our Pain to God: Michael Card and Calvin Seerveld on Biblical Lament in Worship*. June 20, 2008. Accessed October 06, 2016. http://worship.calvin.edu/resources/resource-library/bringing-our-pain-to-god-michael-card-and-calvin-seerveld-on-biblical-lament-in-worship/.

[13] Card, 11.

[14] Card, 12.

Feasting and laughter and pleasure are not wrong, but trying to insulate your life with these things is not really life. It's a bubble. You need to enter the pain of the world around you because the Fall is your reality—"death is the destiny of every man." Take this to heart and you will be wise. Pretend that Christianity is safety from sorrow and you will be a fool.

The way of Christian fellowship is empathy, which means we must not assume that everyone around us is fine. In our conversations, we must listen for complaints and cries and help transform them into laments. In our gathered worship, we must acknowledge the hurting and leave room for struggle and silence. In our counsel, we must pray with and over and for the hurting. This is essential to authentic Christian faith: "Bear one another's burdens, and so fulfill the law of Christ" (Galatians 6:2).

REFLECTION QUESTIONS

1. Who is the Lord bringing to your mind today?
2. How can you move toward them with empathy?

CLOSING PRAYER

As a deer pants for flowing streams, so pants my soul for you, O God. My soul thirsts for God, for the living God. When shall I come and appear before God? My tears have been my food day and night, while they say to me all the day long, "Where is your God?" These things I remember, as I pour out my soul: how I would go with the throng and lead them in procession to the house of God with glad shouts and songs of praise, a multitude keeping festival. Why are you cast down, O my soul, and why are you in turmoil within me? Hope in God; for I shall again praise him, my salvation and my God.

Psalm 42:1–6

Day 28

Daily Readings

CALL TO WORSHIP

Seek the LORD while he may be found; call upon him while he is near; let the wicked forsake his way, and the unrighteous man his thoughts; let him return to the LORD, that he may have compassion on him, and to our God, for he will abundantly pardon. For my thoughts are not your thoughts, neither are your ways my ways, declares the LORD. For as the heavens are higher than the earth, so are my ways higher than your ways and my thoughts than your thoughts.

Isaiah 55:6–9

CONFESSION

Lord, we have not kept watch for you. We have occupied ourselves with our own concerns. We have not waited to find your will for us. We have not noticed the needs of the people around us. We have not acknowledged the love that has been shown to us. Forgive us for our lack of watchfulness. Help us to wait to know your will. Help us to look out for the needs of others. Help us to work and watch for your coming. Amen.[1]

GOSPEL OF MARK

But concerning that day or that hour, no one knows, not even the angels in heaven, nor the Son, but only the Father. Be on guard, keep awake. For you do not know when the time will come. It is like a man going on a journey, when he leaves home and puts his servants in

---

[1] *The Worship Sourcebook*, 443.

charge, each with his work, and commands the doorkeeper to stay awake. Therefore stay awake—for you do not know when the master of the house will come, in the evening, or at midnight, or when the rooster crows, or in the morning— lest he come suddenly and find you asleep. And what I say to you I say to all: Stay awake.

Mark 13:32–37

PRAYER OF THANKSGIVING

Gracious Lord, in our helpless state, you draw near to us—we give you thanks. Compassionate Father, in our sin and despair, you abundantly pardon—we give you thanks. Almighty God, your ways are higher than our ways—we give you praise.

Daily Devotion

Cast me not away from your presence, and take not your Holy Spirit from me. Restore to me the joy of your salvation, and uphold me with a willing spirit.

Psalm 51:11–12

The deepest longing of our soul is the all-satisfying *hesed* of God—not in the abstract, but in firsthand experience. To taste God is to see that he is good (Psalm 34:8). Just one day in his presence is better than any number of days anywhere else (Psalm 84:10). We have experienced moments of God's presence and power, and we feel a sense of longing in between those moments.

Now consider Jesus, who enjoyed unbroken fellowship with God. How devastating was his longing, and how deep his pain when he took upon the judgment of God on the cross? All lament leads us to Jesus, in whom our sorrow and pain finds ultimate identification and hope.

The apex of bewilderment and spiritual chaos for Jesus was on the cross. The physical pain was excruciating, yet it was nothing compared to the shock and horror of being forsaken by the Father. The wrath of God was poured out on Jesus, the whole weight of the world's guilt bearing down on his shoulders. He felt the pain and loss of humanity. He internalized our anger and shame. God made him who knew no sin, to become sin (2 Corinthians 5:21).

In that moment, he took up the lament of King David: "My God, my God, why have you forsaken me?" (Mark 15:34). When he said this he not only took our sin upon himself, but also voiced our laments. For underlying all our laments are two questions: "God, where are you?" and, "God, if you love me, then why?" For the first time in all of eternity, Jesus felt the absence of the Father's presence.

Why did it have to be this way? If Jesus was God's answer to ages of laments, how did he end up in the most lamentable position of all?

One approach to the question is to consider why so many ultimately rejected him, even his own people (John 1:11). They had expectations about what it would mean for God to answer their prayers and solve their problems. The disciples, too, regularly stumbled over their expectations. They hoped the Messiah would conquer the Romans and vindicate Israel. Instead, he predicted the destruction of the temple and died at the hand of the Romans.

They wanted the Messiah to give them answers. Jesus gave himself. He predicted his own destruction, and then endured it in order to conquer our real enemies: Satan, sin, and death. Jesus did not take away lamenting. He took it up. Having endured the cross, he secured for us the one thing we need more than solutions: the presence of God. He sent the Holy Spirit to indwell us and interceded for us, so that nothing could separate us from the love of God (Romans 8:26–39).

REFLECTION QUESTIONS

1. Make a list of what Jesus endured on the cross for our sakes. Have you also lamented as you have endured some of the same? How does knowing that Jesus suffered in the same ways encourage you?
2. What would be some of the differences between your suffering and Jesus's suffering? Will God ever ask you to suffer without his presence?
3. How could the presence of God be more satisfying to you than any "solutions" to your problems?

CLOSING PRAYER

So teach us to number our days that we may get a heart of wisdom. Return, O LORD! How long? Have pity on your servants! Satisfy us in the morning with your steadfast love, that we may rejoice and be glad all our days. Make us glad for as many days as you have afflicted us, and for as many years as we have seen evil. Let your work be shown to your servants, and your glorious power to their children. Let the favor of the Lord our God be upon us, and establish the work of our hands upon us; yes, establish the work of our hands!

Psalm 90:12–17

FIFTH SUNDAY OF LENT

The Lord Jesus was born under the law and perfectly fulfilled it. He endured most grievous torments in his soul and most painful sufferings in his body; he was crucified, died, and was buried; he remained under the power of death, yet his body did not undergo decay; and he arose from the dead on the third day with the same body in which he had suffered. In this body he ascended into heaven, where he sits at the right hand of his Father, making intercession, and he shall return to judge men and angels at the end of the age. The Lord Jesus, by his perfect obedience and sacrifice of himself—which he through the eternal Spirit once offered up to God—has fully satisfied the justice of his Father. He purchased not only reconciliation but also an everlasting inheritance in the kingdom of heaven for all whom the Father has given to him.[2]

> *Christ is risen! Hallelujah! Risen our victorious head!*
> *Sing his praises! Hallelujah! Christ is risen from the dead!*
> *Gratefully our hearts adore him as his light once more appears,*
> *bowing down in joy before him, rising up from griefs and tears.*
>
> *Christ is risen! All the sadness of our Lenten fast is o'er;*
> *through the open gates of gladness he returns to life once more;*
> *death and hell before him bending see him rise, the victor now,*
> *angels on his steps attending, glory round his wounded brow.*
>
> *Christ is risen! All the sorrow that last evening round him lay*
> *now hath found a glorious morrow in the rising of today,*
> *See the grave its first-fruits giving, springing up from holy ground;*
> *Christ was dead, but now is living; he was lost, but he is found.*
>
> *Christ is risen! Henceforth never death or hell shall us enthrall.*
> *We are Christ's, in him forever we have triumphed over all.*
> *All the doubting and dejection of our trembling hearts have ceased;*
> *hail the day of resurrection! Let us rise and keep the feast.*[3]

---

[2] Westminster Confession of Faith, Chapter 8.
[3] John Monsell, Christ is Risen! Hallelujah!, 1863.

WEEK FIVE: SACRIFICE

Day 29

Daily Readings

CALL TO WORSHIP

The LORD our God, the LORD is one. <u>You shall love the LORD your God with all your heart</u> and with all your soul and with all your might. And these words that I command you today shall be on your heart. <u>You shall teach them diligently to your children</u>, and shall <u>talk of them</u> when <u>you sit</u> in your house, and when <u>you walk</u> by the way, and when <u>you lie down,</u> and <u>when you rise</u>. You shall bind them as a sign on your hand, and they shall be as frontlets between your eyes. You shall write them on the doorposts of your house and on your gates. <u>It is the LORD your God you shall fear</u>. Him you shall serve and by his name you shall swear. You shall not go after other gods, the gods of the peoples who are around you—for the <u>LORD your God in your midst is a jealous God</u>—lest the anger of the LORD your God be kindled against you, and he destroy you from off the face of the earth.

Deuteronomy 6:4–9; 13–15

CONFESSION

God of love, it is your will that we should love you with all of our heart, soul, mind, strength, and our neighbor as ourselves, but we are not sufficient for these things. We confess that our affections continually turn away from you: from purity to lust, from freedom to slavery, from compassion to indifference, from fullness to emptiness. Have mercy on us. Order our lives by your holy Word, and make your commandments the joy of our hearts. Conform us to the image of your loving Son Jesus that we may shine before the world to your glory. Amen.

GOSPEL OF MARK

It was now two days before the Passover and the Feast of Unleavened Bread. And the chief priests and the scribes were seeking how to arrest him by stealth and kill him, for they said, "Not during the feast, lest there be an uproar from the people." And while he was at Bethany in the house of Simon the leper, as he was reclining at table, a woman came with an alabaster flask of ointment of pure nard, very costly, and she broke the flask and poured it over his head. There were some who said to themselves indignantly, "Why was the ointment wasted like that? For this ointment could have been sold for more than three hundred denarii and given to the poor." And they scolded her. But Jesus said, "Leave her alone. Why do you trouble her? She has done a beautiful thing to me. For you always have the poor with you, and whenever you want, you can do good for them. But you will not always have me. She has done what she could; she has anointed my body beforehand for burial. And truly, I say to you, wherever the gospel is proclaimed in the whole world, what she has done will be told in memory of her."

Mark 14:1–9

PRAYER OF THANKSGIVING

You are worthy, our Lord and God, to receive all blessing and honor and praise, and you are sufficient for us in all things. Thank you for mouths to praise you, for feet to walk in your ways, and for hearts to cherish and worship you.

Daily Devotion

I will greatly rejoice in the LORD; my soul shall exult in my God, for he has clothed me with the garments of salvation; he has covered me with the robe of righteousness.

Isaiah 61:10

After sin entered the world and God pronounced his judgment on Adam and Eve, we read in Genesis 3:21: "And the LORD God made for Adam and for his wife garments of skins and clothed them."

God looked at their hastily made clothes and said, "Nope. That's not going to work." The clothes that Adam and Eve made for themselves were not adequate covering to face the new fallen world in which they were now living. Remember when they first sinned? Sin opened their eyes, but not in a good way. Sin laid them bare, left them feeling exposed. For the first time, they realized they were naked. So, they sewed fig leaves together and made themselves loincloths, single-piece garments. And ever since, the human race has engaged in an enterprise of self-covering that always falls short.

God knew that Adam and Eve needed something more substantial for covering. They needed something made by his hands, not their own. When we read Genesis 3:21, it is apparent that some animals had to die in order that the man and woman could be sufficiently clothed. This is the first hint of substitutionary atonement that we see in the Bible. "Substitutionary atonement" is just a fancy way of saying that an innocent one died so that a guilty one could be covered. You see, covering sin is not simple, quick, and easy (like grabbing some leaves off a tree and sewing them together). Covering sin is costly, painful . . . bloody. Sin produces suffering and death, so the cost of covering sin involves suffering and death. It involves sacrifice.

Did Adam and Eve think they could just sweep things under the rug, tidy up the disastrous mess they had made without any cost, without any price being paid? Do we think that? When we try to cover our own sin, we are engaging in a futile self-salvation project. We are essentially saying, "I can atone for my own sin." But this is a gross underestimation of both the breadth and depth of sin's devastation.

The death of the animals in Genesis 3 is the first biblical hint that atonement requires sacrifice. It points us forward to the ultimate sacrifice. Jesus Christ suffered and bled and died so that we could be adequately clothed—clothed in his righteousness. The blood of Jesus is our atonement, our covering. Just like Adam and Eve, we can't cover our own sin. God must do that, and he has made that possible with the costly sacrifice of his own Son.

REFLECTION QUESTIONS

1. What are some of your fig leaves (false coverings)? These are just things you and I use to try to make ourselves look okay or feel okay about ourselves (good works, talents and abilities, religious duty and discipline, performance at work).
2. God calls us to put our faith in the covering that he alone provides. He calls us to faith in Christ. The bloody death of Jesus is our only hope. What would it look like for you to believe that today when you are tempted to "self-cover"?

CLOSING PRAYER

Everlasting Creator-Father, I bless thee for the everlasting covenant, for the appointment of a Mediator. I rejoice that he failed not, nor was discouraged, but accomplished the work thou gavest him to do; and said on the cross, "It is finished." I exult in the thought that thy justice is satisfied, thy truth established, thy law magnified, and a foundation is laid for my hope. I look to a present and personal interest in Christ and say, surely he has borne my griefs, carried my sorrows, won my peace, healed my soul. Justified by his blood I am saved by his life, glorying in his cross I bow to his scepter, having his Spirit I possess his mind. Lord, grant that my religion may not be occasional and partial, but universal, influential, effective, and may I always continue in thy words as well as thy works, so that I may reach my end in peace.[4]

---

[4] *The Valley of Vision*, 72–73.

Day 30

Daily Readings

CALL TO WORSHIP

Clap your hands, all peoples! Shout to God with loud songs of joy! For the LORD, the Most High, is to be feared, a great king over all the earth. He subdued peoples under us, and nations under our feet. He chose our heritage for us, the pride of Jacob whom he loves. Selah. God has gone up with a shout, the LORD with the sound of a trumpet. Sing praises to God, sing praises! Sing praises to our King, sing praises! For God is the King of all the earth; sing praises with a psalm! God reigns over the nations; God sits on his holy throne. The princes of the peoples gather as the people of the God of Abraham. For the shields of the earth belong to God; he is highly exalted!

Psalm 47

CONFESSION

Almighty God, who is rich in mercy to all those who call upon you; hear us as we come to you humbly confessing our sins, and asking for your mercy and forgiveness. We have broken your holy laws by our deeds and by our words, and by the sinful affections of our heart. We confess before you our disobedience and ingratitude, our pride and willfulness, and all our failures and shortcomings toward you and toward our family and friends. Have mercy upon us, most merciful Father, and through your great goodness grant that we may from now on serve and please you in newness of life; grant us this, we pray, through the mediation of Jesus Christ our Savior and Lord. Amen.

GOSPEL OF MARK

Then Judas Iscariot, who was one of the twelve, went to the chief priests in order to betray him to them. And when they heard it, they were glad and promised to give him money. And he sought an opportunity to betray him. And on the first day of Unleavened Bread, when they sacrificed the Passover lamb, his disciples said to him, "Where will you have us go and prepare for you to eat the Passover?" And he sent two of his disciples and said to them, "Go into the city, and a man carrying a jar of water will meet you. Follow him, and wherever he enters, say to the master of the house, 'The Teacher says, Where is my guest room, where I may eat the Passover with my disciples?' And he will show you a large upper room furnished and ready; there prepare for us." And the disciples set out and went to the city and found it just as he had told them, and they prepared the Passover. And when it was evening, he came with the twelve. And as they were reclining at table and eating, Jesus said, "Truly, I say to you, one of you will betray me, one who is eating with me." They began to be sorrowful and to say to him one after another, "Is it I?" He said to them, "It is one of the twelve, one who is dipping bread into the dish with me. For the Son of Man goes as it is written of him, but woe to that man by whom the Son of Man is betrayed! It would have been better for that man if he had not been born."

Mark 14:10–21

PRAYER OF THANKSGIVING

Most High God, who reigns over all, we praise you for your sovereign grace and mercy towards us in Christ. Through the mediation of Jesus we find forgiveness. He humbled himself and endured the cross so that we might receive the promised blessings of God. We praise you with songs of joy.

Daily Devotion

Since therefore the children share in flesh and blood, he himself likewise partook of the same things, that through death he might destroy the one who has the power of death, that is, the devil, and deliver all those who through fear of death were subject to lifelong slavery.

Hebrews 2:14–15

Not only was it a sacrifice for God the Son to take on human flesh, you might say that Jesus's entire life was marked by sacrifice—giving up his rights and spending himself for the sake of others. From the beginning of his time on earth, his feet were always walking toward the ultimate sacrifice of death on a brutal Roman cross. This brings a question to mind: Why is sacrifice so central to God's plan of redemption and reconciliation? Why couldn't God just forgive people of their sins without sacrifice?

The short answer is that sin deserves death, and only a sinless sacrifice could satisfy the wrath of God against sin. That said, let's back up and think it through.

If you think about what it means to bring about reconciliation in a human relationship, you can see how sacrifice is always part of the process. Let's say I offend or hurt you in some way. It will cost you something to forgive me, because you will have to absorb the pain of the offense. You will have to sacrifice your right to be angry and move toward me with forgiveness. But I will have to sacrifice too. I will have to lay down my pride if I am going to move toward you with confession and repentance. The bottom line is that without sacrifice there is no reconciliation. There is only hardness of heart and death of relationship.

In a very similar way, we must sacrifice in order to move toward God with confession and repentance. We must come to the end of ourselves, killing any sense of pride and self-righteousness. But we are not the ones who move first. It is not our sacrifice that saves us. God's plan of redemption is primarily about his sacrifice, not ours.

Redemption is a term of value, so there must be a cost involved. To redeem means to buy back, to regain possession of something in exchange for payment. The cost of redeeming a human being is staggering. What does it cost to buy a person back from the realm of sin and death, from the reign of Satan? The payment is commensurate with the destruction that sin, death, and Satan have brought to humanity. No amount of sacrifice on our part would enable us to cover the cost. Thankfully, the full cost fell on Jesus. All of the curses of the Fall—our sins and the resulting death—were placed on Christ. His sacrifice makes our reconciliation with God possible. Thanks be to God!

REFLECTION QUESTIONS

1. Is there anyone in your life with whom you need to reconcile? If they are in the wrong, what will it cost you to forgive them? If you are in the wrong, what will it cost you to ask their forgiveness? How do you think those costs compare to what it cost Jesus to buy your forgiveness?

2. Spend a few moments thanking God for the sacrifice of his Son to buy your redemption. Thank him for paying for specific sins for which you could never have paid.

CLOSING PRAYER

Send your Spirit among us, O God, as we meditate on the sacrifice of Jesus Christ. Prepare our minds to hear your Word. Move our hearts to accept what we hear. Purify our will to obey in joy and faith. This we pray through Christ, our Savior. Amen.[5]

---

[5] *The Worship Sourcebook*, 570.

Day 31

Daily Readings

CALL TO WORSHIP

Praise the LORD! I will give thanks to the LORD with my whole heart, in the company of the upright, in the congregation. Great are the works of the LORD, studied by all who delight in them. Full of splendor and majesty is his work, and his righteousness endures forever. He has caused his wondrous works to be remembered; the LORD is gracious and merciful. He provides food for those who fear him; he remembers his covenant forever. He has shown his people the power of his works, in giving them the inheritance of the nations. The works of his hands are faithful and just; all his precepts are trustworthy; they are established forever and ever, to be performed with faithfulness and uprightness. He sent redemption to his people; he has commanded his covenant forever. Holy and awesome is his name! The fear of the LORD is the beginning of wisdom; all those who practice it have a good understanding. His praise endures forever!

Psalm 111

CONFESSION

Eternal God, whose covenant with us is never broken: We confess that we have failed to fulfill your will for us. We betray our neighbors, desert our friends, and run in fear when we should be loyal. Though you have bound yourself to us, we have not bound ourselves to you. God, have mercy on us weak and willful people. Lead us once again to your table, and unite us to Christ, who is the bread of life and the vine from which we grow in grace. To Christ be praise forever. Amen.[6]

[6] *The Worship Sourcebook*, 598.

GOSPEL OF MARK

And as they were eating, he took bread, and after blessing it broke it and gave it to them, and said, "Take; this is my body." And he took a cup, and when he had given thanks he gave it to them, and they all drank of it. And he said to them, "This is my blood of the covenant, which is poured out for many. Truly, I say to you, I will not drink again of the fruit of the vine until that day when I drink it new in the kingdom of God." And when they had sung a hymn, they went out to the Mount of Olives. And Jesus said to them, "You will all fall away, for it is written, 'I will strike the shepherd, and the sheep will be scattered.' But after I am raised up, I will go before you to Galilee." Peter said to him, "Even though they all fall away, I will not." And Jesus said to him, "Truly, I tell you, this very night, before the rooster crows twice, you will deny me three times." But he said emphatically, "If I must die with you, I will not deny you." And they all said the same.

Mark 14:22–31

PRAYER OF THANKSGIVING

Thank you God for not deserting or betraying your covenant with us. Thank you for forgiving our faithlessness and betrayal. Thank you for setting your unconditional love upon us. You are our Lord and God.

Daily Devotion

For the Son of God, Jesus Christ, whom we proclaimed among you . . . . was not Yes and No, but in him it is always Yes. For all the promises of God find their Yes in him. That is why it is through him that we utter our Amen to God for his glory. And it is God who establishes us with you in Christ, and has anointed us, and who has also put his seal on us and given us his Spirit in our hearts as a guarantee.

2 Corinthians 1:19–22

Can we know for sure that God keeps his promises? Everyone knows how easy it is to make a verbal promise, but then waffle on it when it becomes difficult to keep. Could this ever happen with God?

In Genesis, God made a series of promises to Abraham: He promised to give Abraham many descendants and make him into a great nation, to bless him and make his name great, and to bless all the families of the earth through him. He also promised to give the descendants of Abraham a particular land. But Abraham was unsure. His circumstances didn't indicate that God's promises could actually come to fruition. So, in Genesis 15, Abraham asked God some questions: "O Lord GOD, what will you give me, for I continue childless," and, "O Lord GOD, how am I to know that I shall possess [the land]" (15:2, 8)?

In answer to these questions, God did something that seems strange to us in our cultural context. He had Abraham sacrifice some animals, cut them in half, and then lay the pieces of the animals across from each other. Then Abraham fell into a deep sleep, and a smoking fire pot and flaming torch passed between the pieces. This ceremony, common in the ancient Near East, was called "cutting a covenant." Two parties entering into a binding agreement or covenant with one another would cut an animal in pieces and pass between the pieces to inaugurate the covenant. The ceremony signified that the two parties were promising to fulfill the terms of the covenant. If they failed to keep the promises of the covenant, they were saying, "May we become like this animal." It's like they were saying, "I promise. Cross my heart and hope to die." The sacrificial ceremony was literally a pledge of one's life to keep the promises of the covenant.

When the smoking fire pot and flaming torch (which were symbols of God's presence) passed between the pieces of dead animals, God himself was assuming responsibility to make sure that all the promises of the covenant were kept. Abraham was asleep, completely passive, while God initiated and ratified the covenant. O. Palmer Robertson writes, "The solemn ceremony of self-malediction provides the Lord's reply [to Abraham's questions]: 'I promise. I solemnly commit myself as Almighty God. Death may be necessary. But the promises of the covenant shall be fulfilled.'"

It's a staggering thought! God was saying, "May I be torn to pieces like these animals if the covenant between me and Abraham's descendants is broken." The terms of the covenant would end up being broken—but not by God.

Abraham's descendants would be unfaithful to God and his covenant. But God kept his promise. He had sworn on his life to bless Abraham. So, the blessing for Abraham and his descendants (which includes us as Christians) was made possible by the curse of death that fell on Jesus. In Jesus, God the Son took on flesh, and his flesh was torn apart in order to keep his covenant promises to Abraham (and us). Jesus, the covenant-keeper, sacrificially offered himself for us: Take, eat; this is my body. Drink of this cup, all of you, for this is my blood of the covenant, which is poured out for many for the forgiveness of sins (Matthew 26:26–28). The blood of Jesus, the sacrificial Lamb of God, is our assurance that God keeps his promises.

REFLECTION QUESTIONS

1. What promises of God (which you have in Christ) are you struggling to believe? How can the blood of Christ give you assurance that God keeps his promises to his children?
2. Spend a few moments praising God for his covenant-keeping and thanking him for fulfilling all the provisions of the covenant that bind you in everlasting relationship with him.

CLOSING PRAYER

O Christ, by remaining faithful till death, you show us the road to greater love. O Christ, by taking the burden of sin upon yourself, you reveal to us the way of generosity. O Christ, by praying for those who crucified you, you lead us to forgive without counting the cost. O Christ, by opening paradise to the repentant thief, you awaken hope in us. O Christ, come and help our weak faith. O Christ, create a pure heart in us; renew and strengthen our spirit. O Christ, your Word is near; may it live within us and protect us always. Amen.[7]

---

[7] *The Worship Sourcebook*, 570.

Day 32

Daily Readings

CALL TO WORSHIP

The Lord who calls us to worship today is the same Jesus who refused the temptation to worship the evil one. Rather than receive the glorious kingdoms of this world, he endured the shame of the cross, and today is Lord of lords and King of kings. Now are gathered in him all the treasures of wisdom and knowledge, glory and power. With the saints of all ages we say, "Worthy is the Lamb who was slain, to receive power and wealth and wisdom and might and honor and glory and blessing!"

Based on Colossians 2:3; Revelation 5:12

CONFESSION

Almighty God, who knows all and sees all: We confess our constant striving for righteousness, acceptance, and approval from sources that leave us empty. We ask your forgiveness, and we renew our hope in Christ alone, who offered himself to appease your wrath and forgive our sins. We find all comfort in his wounds, and we have no need to seek or invent any other means to reconcile ourselves with God, than this one and only sacrifice which renders believers perfect forever.[8]

GOSPEL OF MARK

And they went to a place called Gethsemane. And he said to his disciples, "Sit here while I pray." And he took with him Peter and James and John, and began to be greatly distressed and troubled.

---

[7] Adapted from the Belgic Confession, Art. 21.

And he said to them, "My soul is very sorrowful, even to death. Remain here and watch." And going a little farther, he fell on the ground and prayed that, if it were possible, the hour might pass from him. And he said, "Abba, Father, all things are possible for you. Remove this cup from me. Yet not what I will, but what you will." And he came and found them sleeping, and he said to Peter, "Simon, are you asleep? Could you not watch one hour? Watch and pray that you may not enter into temptation. The spirit indeed is willing, but the flesh is weak." And again he went away and prayed, saying the same words. And again he came and found them sleeping, for their eyes were very heavy, and they did not know what to answer him. And he came the third time and said to them, "Are you still sleeping and taking your rest? It is enough; the hour has come. The Son of Man is betrayed into the hands of sinners. Rise, let us be going; see, my betrayer is at hand."

Mark 14:32–42

PRAYER OF THANKSGIVING

Lord Jesus, we thank you for reconciling us to God. You are the perfect atoning sacrifice that brings us forgiveness and salvation. You carried your own cross and there you were slain, cancelling our debt. You are the worthy Lamb!

Daily Devotion

[God] said [to Abraham], "Take your son, your only son Isaac, whom you love, and go to the land of Moriah, and offer him there as a burnt offering on one of the mountains of which I shall tell you." So Abraham rose early in the morning, saddled his donkey, and took two of his young men with him, and his son Isaac. And he cut the wood for the burnt offering and arose and went to the place of which God had told him.

Genesis 22:2–3

It's hard to imagine the complexity of emotions Abraham must have had as he made his way up Mount Moriah, the place where God had commanded him to sacrifice his beloved son. Isaac was his only begotten (i.e. unique, special) child, the one he had waited decades for, the one whom God had promised and then miraculously provided. Isaac was a physical sign of God's goodness and faithfulness to keep his covenant with Abraham. He represented all the dreams and aspirations of Abraham's heart—Isaac was Abraham's treasure. There was a lot at stake.

We don't know exactly what Abraham was feeling, but we do know how he responded. Instead of arguing with God, he immediately began preparing for the sacrifice. His response was obedience: he "saddled his donkey," "cut wood for the burnt offering," and began making his way up the mountain. In the face of great cost, Abraham obeyed.

This isn't like the man in Jesus's parable who found a treasure in a field and sold everything he had to buy the field. That man knew what he stood to gain—he had good reason to be confident in the reward that awaited him. Sacrifice comes more easily when we are assured of the payoff. But Abraham had no such assurance, just a mysterious faith that he and his son would come back together from the altar (22:5).

When they came to the altar, Abraham carefully laid out the wood, then bound his son Isaac and placed him on top. Then suddenly, just as he was taking the knife to slaughter his son, God interceded:

"But the angel of the LORD called to him from heaven and said, "Abraham, Abraham!' And he said, 'Here I am.' He said, 'Do not lay your hand on the boy or do anything to him, for now I know that you fear God, seeing you have not withheld your son, your only son, from me.' And Abraham lifted up his eyes and looked, and behold, behind him was a ram, caught in a thicket by his horns. And Abraham went and took the ram and offered it up as a burnt offering instead of his son" (22:11–13).

To believe God means to trust beyond reason and reward that he is good, and that what he demands he also provides. It is in this sense that Abraham believed God, and so was willing to obey God, even to the point of offering up his only begotten son.

God honors our obedience and worship by providing what we really want and desperately need: a substitutionary sacrifice. Abraham did not withhold his only son from God; "[God] did not spare his own Son but gave him up for us all" (Romans 8:32). Isaac was the promised seed of Abraham through whom God would bless the nations; Jesus was the promised seed of Adam through whom God would bring redemption to all peoples throughout history. Isaac carried the wood on his back up to the altar to be sacrificed; Jesus carried his own cross on the road to Calvary where he would be crucified. Isaac was laid upon the altar in anticipation of his death through his father's own hand; Jesus was slain upon the altar and cut off from his Father. A substitutionary lamb was provided for Isaac, but Jesus was the substitutionary lamb provided for us all.

Jesus is the greater and perfect sacrifice who empowers our obedience and worship.

REFLECTION QUESTIONS

1. What is your treasure, the thing you cherish and protect and want to control?
2. What would it look like for you to "give" that to God?
3. Can you trust his goodness and provision for you?

CLOSING PRAYER

O God of Abraham, Isaac and Jacob, all that were ever saved were saved by thee, and will through eternity exclaim, "Not unto us, but unto thy name give glory for thy mercy and truth's sake." Thou hast chosen to transact all thy concerns with us through a Mediator in whom all fullness dwells and who is exalted to be Prince and Saviour. To him we look, on him we depend, through him we are justified. May we derive relief from his sufferings without ceasing to abhor sin, or to long after holiness; feel the double efficacy of his blood, tranquilizing and cleansing our consciences; delight in his service as well as in his sacrifice.[9]

---

[9] *The Valley of Vision*, 400–401.

Day 33

Daily Readings

CALL TO WORSHIP

The LORD works righteousness and justice for all who are oppressed. He made known his ways to Moses, his acts to the people of Israel. The LORD is merciful and gracious, slow to anger and abounding in steadfast love. He will not always chide, nor will he keep his anger forever. He does not deal with us according to our sins, nor repay us according to our iniquities. For as high as the heavens are above the earth, so great is his steadfast love toward those who fear him; as far as the east is from the west, so far does he remove our transgressions from us. As a father shows compassion to his children, so the LORD shows compassion to those who fear him.

Psalm 103:6–13

CONFESSION

O God, from ages past no ear has heard, and no eye has seen any God besides you, who works for those who wait for him. But we have all become like one who is unclean, and all our righteous deeds are like filthy garments. We all fade like a leaf, and our iniquities, like the wind, take us away. Yet you, O Lord, are our Father; we are the clay, and you are the potter; we are the work of your hand. Do not be exceedingly angry, O Lord, and do not remember our sin forever. Restore us, we pray, through the grace of our Lord Jesus, in whom we place our hope and trust, (Based on Isaiah 64)

GOSPEL OF MARK

And immediately, while he was still speaking, Judas came, one of the twelve, and with him a crowd with swords and clubs, from the chief priests and the scribes and the elders. Now the betrayer had given them a sign, saying, "The one I will kiss is the man. Seize him and lead him away under guard." And when he came, he went up to him at once and said, "Rabbi!" And he kissed him. And they laid hands on him and seized him. But one of those who stood by drew his sword and struck the servant of the high priest and cut off his ear. And Jesus said to them, "Have you come out as against a robber, with swords and clubs to capture me? Day after day I was with you in the temple teaching, and you did not seize me. But let the Scriptures be fulfilled." And they all left him and fled. And a young man followed him, with nothing but a linen cloth about his body. And they seized him, but he left the linen cloth and ran away naked.

Mark 14:43–52

PRAYER OF THANKSGIVING

Merciful and gracious Lord, you are slow to anger and abounding in steadfast love. You do not deal with us according to our sins. You have removed our transgressions from us and restored us through the righteousness of your Son, Jesus. Hallelujah, what a Savior!

Daily Devotion

For since the law has but a shadow of the good things to come instead of the true form of these realities, it can never, by the same sacrifices that are continually offered every year, make perfect those who draw near. Otherwise, would they not have ceased to be offered, since the worshipers, having once been cleansed, would no longer have any consciousness of sins? But in these sacrifices there is a reminder of sins every year. For it is impossible for the blood of bulls and goats to take away sins. Consequently, when Christ came into the world, he said, "Sacrifices and offerings you have not desired, but a body have you prepared for me; in burnt offerings and sin offerings you have taken no pleasure. Then I said,

'Behold, I have come to do your will, O God, as it is written of me in the scroll of the book.'"

Hebrews 10:1–7

It is so easy to feel self-righteous about sacrifice. When we "sacrifice" by tithing, or abstaining from sex or alcohol or food, or giving our time to help others, we feel pretty good about ourselves. We might not say it this way, but perhaps we even feel like we have earned some good graces with God. We present these things to God in our minds like we are making a case for why we deserve to be forgiven, or blessed, or noticed. However, this type of thinking prevents us from giving God the sacrifice he desires—after all, our money, our bodies, and our time all belong to him already; is it really so generous to give a small portion back? That is more stewardship than sacrifice.

It will not do to say to God, "Yes, I have sinned, but look what good I have done! Look what I have sacrificed!" God desires a different kind of sacrifice, one that encompasses our very being. In Psalm 51, King David's famous confession concerning his adultery and murder and cover up, he comes clean with God. No excuses, just full disclosure and ownership. No ritual ceremony, just impassioned prayer. This is what people do when they have come to the end of themselves. They bring absolutely nothing to the table, and count on God to be everything to them.

But why didn't David bring this to the altar of ritual worship? He needed forgiveness, and the means of atonement in his day was the blood of an animal. He explains: "For you will not delight in sacrifice, or I would give it; you will not be pleased with a burnt offering. The sacrifices of God are a broken spirit; a broken and contrite heart, O God, you will not despise" (Psalm 51:16–17).

Just as "it is impossible for the blood of bulls and goats to take away sins" (Hebrews 10:4), nothing we sacrifice for God will "tip the scales in our favor" or satisfy his holiness. God alone blots out all our iniquities and restores to us the joy of our salvation (51:9, 12). David's point was not that sacrifices would no longer be made (they would), but simply that a sacrifice in and of itself counts for nothing apart from the heart of the one who offers it.

God desires our whole heart, and the only way to give yourself completely is to let go of the notion that any part of your heart or your spirit or your life is good apart from him. When we stop trying to justify ourselves before God, then our hearts will break as David's did. We will cease striving for a righteousness of our own, stop covering up our unrighteousness, and look only to the sacrifice of Jesus Christ, the Son of God, who "offered for all time a single sacrifice for sins, [and] sat down at the right hand of God." (Hebrews 10:12).

REFLECTION QUESTIONS

1. At what times do you feel like you are doing okay with God? What do you think you are basing that feeling on?
2. How have you judged those around you that do not make the same kind of sacrifices you make for God?
3. What would it take for you to bring nothing to the table (a broken and contrite heart)?

CLOSING PRAYER

Almighty God, giver of every good and perfect gift, teach us to render to you all that we have and all that we are, that we may praise you, not with our lips only, but with our whole lives, turning the duties, the sorrows, and the joys of all our days into a living sacrifice to you, through our Savior, Jesus Christ. Amen.[1]

---

[1] *The Worship Sourcebook*, 244.

Day 34

Daily Readings

CALL TO WORSHIP

The Mighty One, God the Lord, speaks and summons the earth from the rising of the sun to its setting. Out of Zion, the perfection of beauty, God shines forth. Our God comes; he does not keep silence; before him is a devouring fire, around him a mighty tempest. He calls to the heavens above and to the earth, that he may judge his people: "Gather to me my faithful ones, who made a covenant with me by sacrifice!" The heavens declare his righteousness, for God himself is judge!

Psalm 50:1–6

CONFESSION

Merciful God, we meet each other today at the foot of the cross, as inhabitants of one world. We wait with each other as those who inflict wounds on one another: be merciful to us. As those who deny justice to others: be merciful to us. As those who put our trust in power: be merciful to us. As those who are greedy: be merciful to us. As those who put others on trial: be merciful to us. As those who refuse to receive: be merciful to us. As those who are afraid of the world's torment: be merciful to us. Amen.[2]

GOSPEL OF MARK

And they led Jesus to the high priest. And all the chief priests and the elders and the scribes came together. And Peter had followed

---

[2] *The Worship Sourcebook*, 610.

151

him at a distance, right into the courtyard of the high priest. And he was sitting with the guards and warming himself at the fire. Now the chief priests and the whole council were seeking testimony against Jesus to put him to death, but they found none. For many bore false witness against him, but their testimony did not agree. And some stood up and bore false witness against him, saying, "We heard him say, 'I will destroy this temple that is made with hands, and in three days I will build another, not made with hands.'" Yet even about this their testimony did not agree. And the high priest stood up in the midst and asked Jesus, "Have you no answer to make? What is it that these men testify against you?" But he remained silent and made no answer. Again the high priest asked him, "Are you the Christ, the Son of the Blessed?" And Jesus said, "I am, and you will see the Son of Man seated at the right hand of Power, and coming with the clouds of heaven." And the high priest tore his garments and said, "What further witnesses do we need? You have heard his blasphemy. What is your decision?" And they all condemned him as deserving death. And some began to spit on him and to cover his face and to strike him, saying to him, "Prophesy!" And the guards received him with blows.

Mark 14:53–65

PRAYER OF THANKSGIVING

God of justice, you alone are the judge of all the earth. Through Christ's righteous sacrifice you have pardoned us—we the guilty, have gone free. Our hearts are full of gratitude.

Daily Devotion

I appeal to you therefore, brothers, by the mercies of God, to present your bodies as a living sacrifice, holy and acceptable to God, which is your spiritual worship. Do not be conformed to this world, but be transformed by the renewal of your mind, that by testing you may discern what is the will of God, what is good and acceptable and perfect.

Romans 12:1–2

We live in a culture obsessed with self-improvement. We want to change our jobs, bodies, houses, habits, and hobbies. We really want to "improve" the people around us. When it comes to opportunity and options for change, our day is unparalleled in history.

The problem is that we also live in an age of unparalleled convenience. I can shoot a video on my phone and send it to someone on another continent. I can travel across a continent in a few hours. As long as I am willing to pay for it, I can outsource almost any project or need that arises. Privileges like these have cultivated unrealistic expectations and unwarranted impatience.

The Bible offers an entirely different norm for change, which is more profound and deliberate. It promises holistic change, but not all at once, and not without sacrifice. Paul's charge in Romans 12 is to pursue change through sacrifice. For context, Romans 1—11 establishes the sacrifice of Jesus. His death and resurrection, applied to us by the Holy Spirit, is the foundation of real change. In light of those things, we are to present the entirety of who we are to God "as a living sacrifice" to him.

This is a peculiar phrase. The allusion to Old Testament sacrifice is clear, but all those sacrifices died. So what are we to make of this "living sacrifice?"

On one hand, personal growth is sacrificial. We do not need to atone for our sins (Jesus is the final sacrifice for sin), but we do have to put to death our selfish ambition and our desire to be in control. Earlier in Romans, Paul said that those who set their minds on these things are living "according to the flesh" (Romans 8:5), which just means to live according to your own strength. So much of our motive for change is to secure ourselves by our own means. We want to change our bodies to secure a good image, acquire wealth to secure comfort, and gain power to secure our happiness. All of that must be put to death (Galatians 5:24).

That is only part of what Paul is saying here. Our worship is sacrificial, but it is also living: "If by the Spirit you put to death the deeds of the body, you will live" (Romans 8:13). In other words, our sacrifice of worship is to live for God, to present the members of our body to God as "instruments of righteousness" (Romans 6:13). This is possible because "he who raised Christ Jesus from the dead will also give life to [our] mortal bodies through his Spirit who dwells in [us]" (Romans 8:11). Because Jesus offered up his body on the cross to secure our salvation forever, we can offer up our bodies to God as a continual act of worship.

The norm in our culture is to sacrifice whatever we have to get what we want. The way of true sanctification is to sacrifice everything we want because of what we already have in Christ. This is the heart of Lent. We are decluttering our lives, inside and out, testing the values and habits and desires that have become our acceptable norm. We are considering what Jesus gave up for us, and it is changing us.

REFLECTION QUESTIONS

1. What do you want to change about yourself and your life?
2. What would it look like to offer these things to God in worship?
3. How will pursuing change help you seek God above all else?

CLOSING PRAYER

Almighty God, Father of all mercies, we, your unworthy servants, give you humble thanks for all your goodness and loving-kindness to us and to all whom you have made. We bless you for our creation, preservation, and all the blessings of this life, but above all for your immeasurable love in the redemption of the world by our Lord Jesus Christ, for the means of grace, and for the hope of glory. And, we pray, give us such an awareness of your mercies that with truly thankful hearts we may show forth your praise, not only with our lips, but in our lives, by giving up ourselves to your service, and by walking before you in holiness and righteousness all our days, through Jesus Christ, our Lord, to whom, with you and the Holy Spirit, be honor and glory throughout all ages. Amen.[3]

---

[3] *The Worship Sourcebook*, 186.

SIXTH SUNDAY OF LENT: PALM SUNDAY

By his resurrection Christ broke apart the gates of death and opened to us the way of life, announced victory to the women and apostles and brought salvation to the whole world, annihilated the power of death and renewed the entire creation, gave us the promise of resurrection so that we might rise with him in new life. We proclaim and affirm that, through the death and resurrection of Jesus, "Death is swallowed up in victory." And so we cry out: "O death, where is your victory? O death, where is your sting?" The sting of death is sin, and the power of sin is the law. But thanks be to God, who gives us the victory through our Lord Jesus Christ.[4]

Christ Jesus lay in death's strong bands, For our offenses given;
But now at God's right hand He stands, And brings us life from Heaven.
Wherefore let us joyful be, And sing to God right thankfully
Loud songs of Alleluia! Alleluia!

No son of man could conquer death, Such mischief sin had wrought us,
For innocence dwelt not on earth, And therefore death had brought us
Into thralldom from of old, And ever grew more strong and bold
And kept us in his bondage. Alleluia!
But Jesus Christ, God's only Son, To our low state descended,
The cause of death He has undone, His power forever ended,
Ruined all his right and claim, And left him nothing but the name,
His sting is lost forever. Alleluia!

It was a strange and dreadful strife, When life and death contended;
The victory remained with life; The reign of death was ended.
Stripped of power, no more it reigns, An empty form alone remains
Death's sting is lost forever! Alleluia!
Here the true Paschal Lamb we see, Whom God so freely gave us;
He died on the accursed tree—So strong His love!—to save us.
See, His blood doth mark our door; Faith points to it, death passes over,
And Satan cannot harm us. Alleluia!

---

[4] Westminster Confession of Faith Ch. 20.1, and 1 Corinthians 15:55–57

So let us keep the festival, Where to the Lord invites us;
Christ is Himself the joy of all, The sun that warms and lights us.
By His grace He doth impart, Eternal sunshine to the heart;
The night of sin is ended! Alleluia!
Then let us feast this Easter day on the true bread of Heaven;
The Word of grace hath purged away the old and wicked leaven.
Christ alone our souls will feed; He is our meat and drink indeed;
Faith lives upon no other! Alleluia![5]

---

[5] Martin Luther, "Christ Jesus Lay in Death's Strong Bands", 1524.

WEEK SIX: DEATH

Day 35

Daily Readings

CALL TO WORSHIP

On this mountain the Lord of hosts will make for all peoples a feast of rich food, a feast of well-aged wine, of rich food full of marrow, of aged wine well refined. And he will swallow up on this mountain the covering that is cast over all peoples, the veil that is spread over all nations. He will swallow up death forever; and the Lord God will wipe away tears from all faces, and the reproach of his people he will take away from all the earth, for the Lord has spoken. It will be said on that day, "Behold, this is our God; we have waited for him, that he might save us. This is the Lord; we have waited for him; let us be glad and rejoice in his salvation."

Isaiah 25:6–9

CONFESSION

Lord Jesus, like Judas, we have betrayed you; like Peter, we have denied you; and like the other disciples, we have forsaken you. Yet you remain faithful to us unto death, even death on a cross. We plead for your forgiveness and mercy. And we ask that you strengthen us so that we do not turn aside but follow you to the very end—for the final victory belongs to you.[6]

GOSPEL OF MARK

And as Peter was below in the courtyard, one of the servant girls of the high priest came, and seeing Peter warming himself, she looked

---

[6] *The Worship Sourcebook*, 597-598.

at him and said, "You also were with the Nazarene, Jesus." But he denied it, saying, "I neither know nor understand what you mean." And he went out into the gateway and the rooster crowed. And the servant girl saw him and began again to say to the bystanders, "This man is one of them." But again he denied it. And after a little while the bystanders again said to Peter, "Certainly you are one of them, for you are a Galilean." But he began to invoke a curse on himself and to swear, "I do not know this man of whom you speak." And immediately the rooster crowed a second time. And Peter remembered how Jesus had said to him, "Before the rooster crows twice, you will deny me three times." And he broke down and wept.

Mark 14:66–72

PRAYER OF THANKSGIVING

O Lord, despite us turning our backs on you, you invite us to feast on your goodness. You have wiped away our tears and swallowed up death forever. We rejoice in your salvation, O Lord, our God.

Daily Devotion

You foolish person! What you sow does not come to life unless it dies.

1 Corinthians 15:36

Truly, truly, I say to you, unless a grain of wheat falls into the earth and dies, it remains alone; but if it dies, it bears much fruit.

John 12:2

Few things are more negative than death. Death is the end of something— the end of life—bringing with it much defeat and bitterness. Death is to be avoided at all costs.

God in his Word acknowledges death as a terrible enemy, but the Bible also suggests that some kind of death is necessary for life and fruitfulness (1 Corinthians 15 and John 12).

Musician Jon Foreman echoes this same upside-down thinking when he sings, "For these seeds to give birth to life, first they must die."[7] We

[7] Foreman, Jon. "Baptize My Mind," in Spring – EP, lowercase people records, 2008, MP3.

see this every year, all around us as the season of autumn approaches. The leaves change and the flowers fade as the cold grip of death takes hold of them yet again. Old things are dying to bring about new life. It is a strange cycle of mourning and rejoicing that makes up our days. Death brings life, or it at least has that potential.

In many ways, this is the very journey of Lent: death to life. Just as the food we eat must first die in order to sustain our life, so the old self (apart from Christ) must die daily to give birth to the new self. Through the power of the Spirit, we put to death our self-centeredness and we are raised to life in Jesus. We deny ourselves, take up our cross, and follow him. Death brings life.

Death is a looming and scary thing. But the love of God toward us in Christ compels us not to be afraid of death and what it will cost us. God held nothing back, but rather, gave up his own Son for us. Surely he will also return to us life abundantly. And abundant life is this: abiding in Christ. The process of dying to ourselves and our own agenda helps us to locate our treasure (life, joy, purpose) in Jesus. Lent reminds us that true life is found in Jesus.

When the seed of God—Jesus—fell into the ground and died, he gave birth to our redemption and granted us newness of life in him. As we are united with Jesus in his death, we get more of the good life: being with and enjoying Christ! When you truly grasp the death of Jesus, when the truth and beauty of all that Jesus gave up for you sinks into your life, you will joyfully give up all you have and are to follow him.

> *When I survey the wondrous cross*
> *On which the Prince of glory died*
> *My richest gain I count but loss*
> *And pour contempt on all my pride.*
>
> *Were the whole realm of nature mine*
> *That were a present far too small;*
> *Love so amazing, so divine*
> *Demands my soul, my life, my all.*[8]

---

[8] Isaac Watts, "When I Survey the Wondrous Cross," 1707.

REFLECTION QUESTIONS

1. What attitudes, desires, and tendencies toward self-centeredness are present in your life that you need to put to death?
2. In what areas of your life are you unwilling to give up control in order to follow Jesus?
3. What would God have you do this passion week in order to prepare the way for the joy of resurrection that awaits you on Sunday?

CLOSING PRAYER

You are holy, O God of majesty, and blessed is Jesus Christ, your Son, our Lord. As one of us, he knew our joys and sorrows and our struggles with temptation. He was like us in every way except sin. In him we see what you created us to be. Though blameless, he suffered willingly for our sin. Though innocent, he accepted death for the guilty. On the cross he offered himself, a perfect sacrifice, for the life of the world. By his suffering and death, he freed us from sin and death. Risen from the grave, he leads us to the joy of new life. Through Christ, all glory and honor are yours, almighty Father, with the Holy Spirit in the holy church, now and forever. Amen.[9]

---

[9] *The Worship Sourcebook*, 590.

Day 36

Daily Readings

CALL TO WORSHIP

> He is the image of the invisible God, the firstborn of all creation. For by him all things were created, in heaven and on earth, visible and invisible, whether thrones or dominions or rulers or authorities—all things were created through him and for him. And he is before all things, and in him all things hold together. And he is the head of the body, the church. He is the beginning, the firstborn from the dead, that in everything he might be preeminent. For in him all the fullness of God was pleased to dwell, and through him to reconcile to himself all things, whether on earth or in heaven, making peace by the blood of his cross.
>
> Colossians 1:15–20

CONFESSION

Like the people who greeted Jesus as he entered Jerusalem and then later pronounced "Crucify him," we are fickle people who often deny Christ in our thoughts, words, and deeds. Remembering the events of Jesus's last week helps us see ourselves for what we are: sinners in need of a Savior, a Savior—praise God—we have in Christ.[10]

GOSPEL OF MARK

> And as soon as it was morning, the chief priests held a consultation with the elders and scribes and the whole council. And they bound Jesus and led him away and delivered him over to Pilate. And Pilate

---

[10] *The Worship Sourcebook*, 585.

asked him, "Are you the King of the Jews?" And he answered him, "You have said so." And the chief priests accused him of many things. And Pilate again asked him, "Have you no answer to make? See how many charges they bring against you." But Jesus made no further answer, so that Pilate was amazed. Now at the feast he used to release for them one prisoner for whom they asked. And among the rebels in prison, who had committed murder in the insurrection, there was a man called Barabbas. And the crowd came up and began to ask Pilate to do as he usually did for them. And he answered them, saying, "Do you want me to release for you the King of the Jews?" For he perceived that it was out of envy that the chief priests had delivered him up. But the chief priests stirred up the crowd to have him release for them Barabbas instead. And Pilate again said to them, "Then what shall I do with the man you call the King of the Jews?" And they cried out again, "Crucify him." And Pilate said to them, "Why, what evil has he done?" But they shouted all the more, "Crucify him." So Pilate, wishing to satisfy the crowd, released for them Barabbas, and having scourged Jesus, he delivered him to be crucified.

Mark 15:1–15

PRAYER OF THANKSGIVING

We praise you Christ as Lord over all, supreme and sufficient. You are the Word made flesh, full of grace and truth. You were beaten and delivered over to death, and yet death could not hold you. Because you live, we live. We praise you, King Jesus.

Daily Devotion

For freedom Christ has set us free; stand firm therefore, and do not submit again to a yoke of slavery.

Galatians 5:1

The aim during Lent is to identify with Jesus in the wilderness, and to follow him, in some way, through his suffering and persecution and sacrifice. The difficulty in following Jesus, of course, is that the journey leads to the cross.

Nevertheless, we try—to meditate and pray, to give up certain comforts and pleasures to focus our attention, to add other things to live more wisely, to repent of consumerism and take in more of the Bible, more of our relationships, more of serving others . . . we try.

But even in our best efforts, failure is there to greet us. Even in moments of success, pride and self-righteousness lurks.

Six weeks is a long time to pay attention to something. Losing steam comes easily. There are moments when Lent is forgotten altogether, and thoughts begin to creep in: "Lent is just an observance. I don't want to be legalistic, you know." We drift toward the kind of self-justification that is not about enjoying freedom, but rather indulging the flesh (Galatians 5:13).

Then there are other moments, usually when feelings of guilt sink in, when a mindset of performance takes over. We tell ourselves that we really do need to do better at this. We drift toward the kind of determination and comparison that is not about pleasing God, but rather pleasing ourselves (Galatians 5:26).

The constant threat of these two things—license and legalism—is always present in our lives, devilishly waiting to get us off course. Neither produce the fruit of the Spirit (Galatians 5:22–23). Repentance, humility, suffering, lament, and sacrifice do not come naturally. Indulgence and self-righteousness do.

Lent is not hard because we are forgetful or because six weeks is a long time. Lent is hard because we do not want to die. But the way of Jesus leads to the cross. "If anyone would come after me, let him deny himself and take up his cross daily and follow me" (Luke 9:23).

All of our shortcomings related to Lent are but a microcosm of our ragged and duplicitous selves. We are far more sinful than anything we are willing to admit here. Indeed, far worse than we know or could even imagine. But the grace of God in Christ Jesus is far greater and powerful than we have ever dreamed.

Lent is pushing us toward Easter, cultivating a longing for it deep in our hearts. Not a longing to go back to our old ways, but a longing for a Savior, who is faithful even when we are faithless (2 Timothy 2:13).

REFLECTION QUESTIONS

1. What feelings of guilt and/or self-righteousness have crept into your mind during this season?
2. How does the grace of God confront and overcome these thoughts?

CLOSING PRAYER

Holy God, you have opened our ears to hear your Word and our lips to proclaim your truth. Open our eyes this day to see in the cross the revelation of your love; through Jesus the crucified, to whom with you and the Holy Spirit, one God, be honor and praise, now and forever. Amen.[11]

---

[11] *The Worship Sourcebook*, 622.

Day 37

Daily Readings

CALL TO WORSHIP

Long ago, at many times and in many ways, God spoke to our fathers by the prophets, but in these last days he has spoken to us by his Son, whom he appointed the heir of all things, through whom also he created the world. He is the radiance of the glory of God and the exact imprint of his nature, and he upholds the universe by the word of his power. After making purification for sins, he sat down at the right hand of the Majesty on high, having become as much superior to angels as the name he has inherited is more excellent than theirs.

Hebrews 1:1–4

CONFESSION

God our Father, we confess that we fail to live in light of the coming, both past and future, of your Son Jesus Christ. He came to redeem those under the law, but we live as those still under it. You sent the Holy Spirit into our hearts, but we choose instead to live as slaves to our flesh. You purchased our freedom and adopted us as your sons and daughters, but we fail to live out of our identity as your children. Forgive our fear and unbelief. Help us to live as your sons and daughters, heirs to your fatherly blessings, because of what Jesus has done for us. Amen.

GOSPEL OF MARK

And the soldiers led him away inside the palace (that is, the governor's headquarters), and they called together the whole battalion. And they clothed him in a purple cloak, and twisting together a crown of thorns, they put it on him. And they began to salute him, "Hail, King of the Jews!" And they were striking his head with a reed and spitting on him and kneeling down in homage to him. And when they had mocked him, they stripped him of the purple cloak and put his own clothes on him. And they led him out to crucify him.

Mark 15:16–20

PRAYER OF THANKSGIVING

Thank you Lord for purchasing our freedom. We are no longer slaves to our flesh, but we are now children of God and brothers and heirs with Christ, our Savior, who lives and reigns with you and the Spirit.

Daily Devotion

"Death is swallowed up in victory." "O death, where is your victory? O death, where is your sting?" The sting of death is sin, and the power of sin is the law. But thanks be to God, who gives us the victory through our Lord Jesus Christ.

1 Corinthians 15:54–57

Meditating on death, at its very core, is morbid and depressing. We mourn, weep, and lament death, sure—but what is the point of taking a week (at some level six weeks) to meditate and reflect deeply on it? Is that necessary or helpful? Wouldn't it be better to keep things positive?

For the Christian, death is not exclusively bad news because we have a clear view of the grander story. Death isn't the end; it is a movement of the plot that ultimately gives way to the glory of resurrection. Death is no longer a bitter pill to swallow; it has been swallowed up in victory, it has lost its sting. Death is the harbinger of good news for the person who is shaped by God's story. Meditating on death is a means toward understanding the grander story of the gospel.

Amid this grander story, the reality of death confronts and challenges us—it reminds us that life is frail and fleeting, and it beckons us to examine our daily life.

To be a Christian means to have located your identity, your worth, your value in Jesus—he has become your treasure. Death, therefore, serves as a constant reminder of where to place our treasure:

"Do not lay up for yourselves treasures on earth, where moth and rust destroy and where thieves break in and steal, but lay up for yourselves treasures in heaven, where neither moth nor rust destroys and where thieves do not break in and steal. For where your treasure is, there your heart will be also" (Matthew 6:19–21).

A life well lived is one that treasures Christ above all. Meditating on the impending nature and finality of death is necessary because it helps us to examine what we are treasuring.

Meditating on death is also a means toward understanding and receiving the grace of God through Christ. Death is a direct result of the Fall, as sin entered into our reality. Our world—and our own lives—are filled with death and decay because of the power and presence of sin.

We are nearing the end of this Lenten journey. For this journey to become truly real to you, you must come face to face with the depth of sin that is present in your heart and life. You have to see yourself for who you really are: a sinner fully deserving of God's just and holy wrath (Romans 3). We have to see ourselves how God sees us because it is only as we believe what God says about our true condition without him that we will be able to believe what God has done for us to make us his. God has given us his only begotten Son, our true Savior, the Lord Jesus Christ. God has given us his best to redeem us. That is what God has done for us!

God does not ignore our sin; he atones for it. He does not look past who we are, he redeems us through his great love: "In this the love of God was made manifest among us, that God sent his only Son into the world, so that we might live through him. In this is love, not that we have loved God but that he loved us and sent his Son to be the propitiation for our sins" (1 John 4:9–10). Because of the atoning sacrifice of Jesus, we are accepted by God, we are saints in the kingdom of God.

It is only as we believe in the depth of our sin that we can truly understand and believe in the overwhelming grace, mercy, and love of God. And this is the good news of the gospel: God's grace and mercy through the sufficient sacrifice of Jesus on the cross is so much deeper and greater than what we see in our own hearts. Praise Jesus!

REFLECTION QUESTIONS

1. Think back on the past seven days and spend some time confessing specific sins before God.
2. Now reflect on the truth that Jesus went to the cross and died for those very sins. Receive God's forgiveness in Christ, worshiping him for his grace and mercy.

CLOSING PRAYER

Lead us, O God, in the way of Christ. Give us courage to take up our cross and, in full reliance upon your grace, to follow him. Help us to love you above all else and to love our neighbor as we love ourselves, demonstrating that love in deed and word by the power of your Spirit. Give us strength to serve you faithfully until the promised day of resurrection, when, with the redeemed of all the ages, we will feast with you at your table in glory. Through Christ, all glory and honor are yours, almighty Father, with the Holy Spirit in the holy church, now and forever. Amen. [12]

---

[12] *The Worship Sourcebook*, 590.

Day 38:
Maundy Thursday

Daily Readings

CALL TO WORSHIP

I love the LORD, because he has heard my voice and my pleas for mercy. Because he inclined his ear to me, therefore I will call on him as long as I live. The snares of death encompassed me; the pangs of Sheol laid hold on me; I suffered distress and anguish. Then I called on the name of the LORD: "O LORD, I pray, deliver my soul!" Gracious is the LORD, and righteous; our God is merciful. The LORD preserves the simple; when I was brought low, he saved me. Return, O my soul, to your rest; for the LORD has dealt bountifully with you. For you have delivered my soul from death, my eyes from tears, my feet from stumbling; What shall I render to the LORD for all his benefits to me? I will lift up the cup of salvation and call on the name of the LORD, I will pay my vows to the LORD in the presence of all his people.

Psalm 116:1–8; 12–14

CONFESSION

We confess, our Father, that we often fail to live up to our family calling as your new covenant people. We are more ready to resent than to forgive, more ready to manipulate than to serve, more ready to fear than to love, more ready to keep our distance than to welcome, more ready to compete than to help. At the root of this behavior is mistrust. We do not love one another as we should, because we do not believe that you love us as you do. Forgive us our cold unbelief. And make more vivid to us the meaning and depth of your love at the cross. Show us what it cost you to give up your Son that we might become your sons and daughters. We ask this in the name of Jesus our righteousness. Amen.

GOSPEL OF MARK

And they compelled a passerby, Simon of Cyrene, who was coming in from the country, the father of Alexander and Rufus, to carry his cross. And they brought him to the place called Golgotha (which means Place of a Skull). And they offered him wine mixed with myrrh, but he did not take it. And they crucified him and divided his garments among them, casting lots for them, to decide what each should take. And it was the third hour when they crucified him. And the inscription of the charge against him read, "The King of the Jews." And with him they crucified two robbers, one on his right and one on his left. And those who passed by derided him, wagging their heads and saying, "Aha! You who would destroy the temple and rebuild it in three days, save yourself, and come down from the cross!" So also the chief priests with the scribes mocked him to one another, saying, "He saved others; he cannot save himself. Let the Christ, the King of Israel, come down now from the cross that we may see and believe." Those who were crucified with him also reviled him.

Mark 15:21–32

PRAYER OF THANKSGIVING

O Lord Jesus Christ, you are enthroned in heaven, yet you gave up your heavenly perfection to become one of us. We adore you for laying aside your glory and clothing yourself in complete humility as a servant. We praise you, Christ, our King!

Daily Devotion

A new commandment I give to you, that you love one another: just as I have loved you, you also are to love one another. By this all people will know that you are my disciples, if you have love for one another.

John 13:34–35

On Maundy Thursday we remember the last evening Jesus shared with his disciples in the upper room before his arrest and crucifixion. The name "Maundy Thursday" comes from the Latin *mandatum novum,* referring to the "new commandment" Jesus gave his disciples to love one another just as he had loved them. But the disciples do not fully comprehend how deeply Jesus has loved them.

In these last words to his disciples, Jesus is defining what it means to love him. Five times Jesus said that love for him was connected to obeying his commands. And five times he said that his command is that we love each other as he has loved us. The point is unmistakable: our commitment to and love for Jesus is expressed by our love for one another. We are not only united with God in Christ; we are also bound together in Christ, for better or for worse. We married into a family— the family of God. But like the disciples, we do not fully comprehend how deeply Jesus has loved us.

Take in the deep love of God for you through the person of Jesus:

"See what kind of love the Father has given to us, that we should be called children of God; and so we are. . . . In this the love of God was made manifest among us, that God sent his only Son into the world, so that we might live through him. In this is love, not that we have loved God but that he loved us and sent his Son to be the propitiation for our sins" (1 John 3:1, 4:9–10).

"For while we were still weak, at the right time Christ died for the ungodly. For one will scarcely die for a righteous person—though perhaps for a good person one would dare even to die—but God shows his love for us in that while we were still sinners, Christ died for us" (Romans 5:6–8).

"Who shall separate us from the love of Christ? Shall tribulation, or distress, or persecution, or famine, or nakedness, or danger, or sword? As it is written, 'For your sake we are being killed all the day long; we are regarded as sheep to be slaughtered.' No, in all these things we are more than conquerors through him who loved us. For I am sure that neither death nor life, nor angels nor rulers, nor things present nor things to come, nor powers, nor height nor depth, nor anything else in all creation, will be able to separate us from the love of God in Christ Jesus our Lord" (Romans 8:35–39).

God's deep love for us is most powerfully displayed in the death of Jesus on the cross. Love is defined at the cross of Jesus. To the degree that you are able to comprehend and soak in the love of Jesus for you, to the degree that it sinks deep into your fabric—this is the degree to which you will be empowered to carry out the new commandment that Jesus gave to us.

REFLECTION QUESTIONS

1. Ask God to reveal to you the ways in which you do not fully comprehend his love for you. Where do you notice unbelief coloring your thoughts about God's love?
2. Spend a few minutes meditating on the three verses above.

CLOSING PRAYER

Lord Jesus Christ, you stretched out your arms of love on the hard wood of the cross that everyone might come within the reach of your saving embrace: So clothe us in your Spirit that we, reaching forth our hands in love, may bring those who do not know you to the knowledge and love of you, for the honor of your name. Amen.[13]

---

[13] *The Worship Sourcebook*, 603.

Day 39: Good Friday

Daily Readings

CALL TO WORSHIP

Who has believed what he has heard from us? And to whom has the arm of the LORD been revealed? For he grew up before him like a young plant, and like a root out of dry ground; he had no form or majesty that we should look at him, and no beauty that we should desire him. He was despised and rejected by men; a man of sorrows, and acquainted with grief; and as one from whom men hide their faces he was despised, and we esteemed him not. Surely he has borne our griefs and carried our sorrows; yet we esteemed him stricken, smitten by God, and afflicted. But he was pierced for our transgressions; he was crushed for our iniquities; upon him was the chastisement that brought us peace, and with his wounds we are healed. All we like sheep have gone astray; we have turned—every one—to his own way; and the Lord has laid on him the iniquity of us all.

Isaiah 53:1–6

CONFESSION

Gracious God, having heard your Word, we thankfully remember the life of our Lord Jesus Christ on this earth. Yet we also acknowledge our failure to respond earnestly and faithfully to his witness. We often mistake Jesus for a mere earthly king, friendly companion, or problem-solver, failing to see him as the ruler of all creation. We do not appreciate the depth of his passion and sacrifice on the cross, failing to acknowledge him as our way of salvation. Even in this Lenten season, we have not walked faithfully in the way of Jesus Christ. Forgive us, we pray, and bring us ever more fully into the joy of union with Jesus Christ, our Lord. Amen.[14]

GOSPEL OF MARK

And when the sixth hour had come, there was darkness over the whole land until the ninth hour. And at the ninth hour Jesus cried with a loud voice, "Eloi, Eloi, lema sabachthani?" which means, "My God, my God, why have you forsaken me?" And some of the bystanders hearing it said, "Behold, he is calling Elijah." And someone ran and filled a sponge with sour wine, put it on a reed and gave it to him to drink, saying, "Wait, let us see whether Elijah will come to take him down." And Jesus uttered a loud cry and breathed his last. And the curtain of the temple was torn in two, from top to bottom. And when the centurion, who stood facing him, saw that in this way he breathed his last, he said, "Truly this man was the Son of God!" There were also women looking on from a distance, among whom were Mary Magdalene, and Mary the mother of James the younger and of Joses, and Salome. When he was in Galilee, they followed him and ministered to him, and there were also many other women who came up with him to Jerusalem.

Mark 15:33–41

PRAYER OF THANKSGIVING

King of Glory, we adore you, our Savior and Lord. You were pierced and crushed for our sin. You suffered on the cross and gave your life as a ransom for many. It is by your wounds that we are healed. We are filled with joy and gratitude.

Daily Devotion

Again Jesus spoke to them, saying, "I am the light of the world. Whoever follows me will not walk in darkness, but will have the light of life."

John 8:12

---

[14] *The Worship Sourcebook*, 587.

Today is called Good Friday, which is not really good because "good" is too neutral a term. The events of Good Friday are the ultimate paradox—at once atrocious and wonderful, scandalous and beautiful, the worst kind of hate and the best kind of love. On this day we were convicted and pardoned, condemned and freed, cursed and blessed.

It was the darkest day. Many who had followed Jesus up to now fled from the events of Friday. And those who stayed watched in horror: the phony trial, the mob that cried out for the blood of the innocent man, the brutal beating, the savagery of the soldiers, and the grueling walk through the city he had entered to cheers just five days before. Finally, the nails pounded into flesh, the tortured body slouched over, the naked man died as his enemies jeered.

To his disciples—those who had forsaken everything in order to follow Jesus—this day was the opposite of good. This man, in whom they had put all of their hopes, was hanging dead on a tree. This was the death of their faith, the crushing of all their hopes for a new kingdom, and the end of all they believed in. Or so it seemed.

As his followers laid Jesus in the tomb on that same dark day, Easter morning was on the horizon, but on Friday they couldn't see it. They couldn't see the defeat of death, the glory of the resurrection, or the advancement of God's kingdom. They couldn't see the whole story. There was no way around Good Friday, only the way through—through pain and death and burial.

It is the same for us; we cannot get around this day. We must go through the pain and death and burial to get to the resurrection. We must go through the darkness of Good Friday to get to the light of Easter.

God is a God of light: darkness cannot survive in his presence. We, who have dark hearts full of sin, should tremble at this fact. But Jesus, who was completely good, cloaked himself in the darkness of our sin and stood under the wrath of God for us. On the cross, he was destroyed and cut off from his Father. It was to have been our fate. On the first Good Friday, in the midst of our darkest hour, God did not cut us off. Jesus Christ, our true light, plunged himself into the darkness so that we might live in the light.

We can go through the darkness of this day because Jesus went through it before us. He is saving us and bringing about our everlasting joy, in a way only God could have chosen. Easter is not far away!

REFLECTION QUESTIONS

1. Take some time to reflect on the darkness of that first Good Friday. Think about what the disciples must have been experiencing that day.
2. Read back over Isaiah 53:1–6 and Psalm 22. What do you learn in these passages about Good Friday?

CLOSING PRAYER

Holy God, you have opened our ears to hear your Word and our lips to proclaim your truth: open our eyes this day to see in the cross the revelation of your love; through Jesus the crucified, to whom with you and the Holy Spirit, one God, be honor and praise, now and forever. Amen.[15]

---

[15] *The Worship Sourcebook*, 622.

Day 40

Daily Readings

CALL TO WORSHIP

Oh give thanks to the LORD, for he is good; for his steadfast love endures forever! Out of my distress I called on the LORD; the LORD answered me and set me free. The LORD is my strength and my song; he has become my salvation. I shall not die, but I shall live, and recount the deeds of the LORD. The stone that the builders rejected has become the cornerstone. This is the LORD's doing; it is marvelous in our eyes. This is the day that the LORD has made; let us rejoice and be glad in it.

Selected verses from Psalm 118

CONFESSION

Almighty God, in raising Jesus from the grave, you shattered the power of sin and death. We confess that we remain captive to doubt and fear, bound by the ways that lead to death. We confess that we who died to sin still continue to sin. We confess that we have not bowed before Jesus or acknowledged his rule in our lives. We have gone along with the way of the world and failed to give him glory. Forgive us and raise us from sin, that we may be your faithful people, obeying the commands of our Lord Jesus Christ, who rules the world and is head of the church, his body. Amen.[16]

---

[16] *The Worship Sourcebook*, 638.

GOSPEL OF MARK

And when evening had come, since it was the day of Preparation, that is, the day before the Sabbath, Joseph of Arimathea, a respected member of the council, who was also himself looking for the kingdom of God, took courage and went to Pilate and asked for the body of Jesus. Pilate was surprised to hear that he should have already died. And summoning the centurion, he asked him whether he was already dead. And when he learned from the centurion that he was dead, he granted the corpse to Joseph. And Joseph bought a linen shroud, and taking him down, wrapped him in the linen shroud and laid him in a tomb that had been cut out of the rock. And he rolled a stone against the entrance of the tomb. Mary Magdalene and Mary the mother of Joses saw where he was laid.

Mark 15:42–47

PRAYER OF THANKSGIVING

Thank you God for answering us and setting us free in Christ Jesus. He is the cornerstone of our faith: He is our strength, our song, and our salvation. In Christ, we are forgiven! Thanks be to God.

Daily Devotion

And I heard a loud voice from the throne saying, "Behold, the dwelling place of God is with man. He will dwell with them, and they will be his people, and God himself will be with them as their God. He will wipe away every tear from their eyes, and death shall be no more, neither shall there be mourning, nor crying, nor pain anymore, for the former things have passed away."

Revelation 21:3–4

Tomorrow is a celebration. Tomorrow is also the acknowledgement of the "already, but not yet" tension of the gospel. "Already, but not yet" is a phrase that theologians often use to describe the reality of the current age we live in.

On the one hand, the kingdom of God has already come in the person of Jesus. This is good news! As the incarnate God-man, he died on the cross so that through his death and resurrection he might destroy Satan, sin, and death (Hebrews 2:14).

On the other hand, the perfect kingdom toward which he pointed awaits his personal return to earth. Until then, we experience the tension of living between the "already, but not yet" aspects of the kingdom of God. Easter is a celebration of this tension.

There is real life right now for those who trust in Christ: We are new creations (2 Corinthians 5:17–21), we have been saved and made alive with Christ (Ephesians 2:1–10), and as heirs with Christ we have received the Spirit of adoption as sons of God (Romans 8:12–17).

And yet there is far more to come for those who trust in Christ: We will have new bodies (1 Corinthians 15:35–49), we will be resurrected like Christ (Romans 6:4–5), and we will experience glorification as children of God (Romans 8:18–30).

The salvation that God brings is here! It is finished, and it is coming. Our hope is in Jesus who accomplished for us the "already, and yet to come." Jesus, through his death, has already delivered his people from slavery to sin. Jesus, through his resurrection, has already conquered death, our worst enemy. But Jesus has not yet allowed us to experience a world without sin, death, and brokenness. He has not yet established his kingdom in full. His promise is to come back and do so.

Until then, we walk by faith in him. We look in hope to his coming, knowing that God does not fail to deliver on his promises. Because he was faithful in the already, we can trust that he will be faithful in the not yet. Jesus has inaugurated the reign of God so that the age to come has invaded the present age. One day, however, at the appointed time, the present age will finally give way to the fullness and completeness of the rule of God in Christ. He will usher in his kingdom in full—a new earth where only righteousness dwells. A land of promise—where there is life, abundance, satisfaction, delight, and rest.

REFLECTION QUESTIONS

1. How have you seen God work in your heart and mind through this journey of Lent?

2. In what areas of your life do you most long to experience greater transformation through the victory of Easter?

CLOSING PRAYER

Giver of life, we wait with you to offer the hope that comes from the cross to earth's darkest places. Where pain is deep and affection is denied, let love break through. Where justice is destroyed, let sensitivity to right spring up. Where hope is crucified, let faith persist. Where peace has no chance, let passion live on. Where truth is trampled underfoot, let the struggle continue. Where fear paralyzes, let forgiveness break through. Eternal God, reach into the silent darkness of our souls with the radiance of the cross. O you who are the bearer of all pain, have mercy on us. Giver of life, have mercy on us. Merciful God, have mercy on us. Amen.[17]

---

[17] *The Worship Sourcebook*, 619.

EASTER SUNDAY

When the Sabbath was past, Mary Magdalene, Mary the mother of James, and Salome bought spices, so that they might go and anoint him. And very early on the first day of the week, when the sun had risen, they went to the tomb. And they were saying to one another, "Who will roll away the stone for us from the entrance of the tomb?" And looking up, they saw that the stone had been rolled back—it was very large. And entering the tomb, they saw a young man sitting on the right side, dressed in a white robe, and they were alarmed. And he said to them, "Do not be alarmed. You seek Jesus of Nazareth, who was crucified. He has risen; he is not here. See the place where they laid him. But go, tell his disciples and Peter that he is going before you to Galilee. There you will see him, just as he told you." And they went out and fled from the tomb, for trembling and astonishment had seized them, and they said nothing to anyone, for they were afraid. (Mark 16:1–8)

> *Christ, the Lord, is risen today, Alleluia!*
> *Sons of men and angels say, Alleluia!*
> *Raise your joys and triumphs high, Alleluia!*
> *Sing, ye heav'ns, and earth, reply, Alleluia!*
>
> *Love's redeeming work is done, Alleluia!*
> *Fought the fight, the battle won, Alleluia!*
> *Death in vain forbids him rise, Alleluia!*
> *Christ has opened paradise, Alleluia!*
>
> *Lives again our glorious King, Alleluia!*
> *Where, O death, is now thy sting? Alleluia!*
> *Once He died, our souls to save, Alleluia!*
> *Where thy victory, O grave? Alleluia!*

Soar we now where Christ has led, Alleluia!
Following our exalted Head, Alleluia!
Made like Him, like Him we rise, Alleluia!
Ours the cross, the grave, the skies, Alleluia!

Hail, the Lord of earth and heav'n, Alleluia!
Praise to Thee by both be giv'n, Alleluia!
Thee we greet triumphant now, Alleluia!
Hail, the Resurrection Thou, Alleluia![18]

---

[18] Charles Wesley, "Christ the Lord Is Risen Today", 1739.